THE AZRIELI SERIES OF HOLOCAUST SURVIVOR MEMOIRS:
PUBLISHED TITLES

ENGLISH TITLES

Album of My Life by Ann Szedlecki
As The Lilacs Bloomed by Anna Molnár Hegedűs
Bits and Pieces by Henia Reinhartz
A Drastic Turn of Destiny by Fred Mann
E/96: Fate Undecided by Paul-Henri Rips
Fleeing from the Hunter by Marian Domanski
From Generation to Generation by Agnes Tomasov
Gatehouse to Hell by Felix Opatowski
Getting Out Alive by Tommy Dick
The Hidden Package by Claire Baum
If, By Miracle by Michael Kutz
If Home Is Not Here by Max Bornstein
If Only It Were Fiction by Elsa Thon
In Hiding by Marguerite Élias Quddus
Joy Runs Deeper by Bronia and Joseph Beker
Knocking on Every Door by Anka Voticky
Little Girl Lost by Betty Rich
Memories from the Abyss by William Tannenzapf / *But I Had a Happy
   Childhood* by Renate Krakauer
My Heart Is At Ease by Gerta Solan
The Shadows Behind Me by Willie Sterner
Spring's End by John Freund
Suddenly the Shadow Fell by Leslie Meisels with Eva Meisels
Survival Kit by Zuzana Sermer
Tenuous Threads by Judy Abrams / *One of the Lucky Ones*
   by Eva Felsenburg Marx
Traces of What Was by Steve Rotschild
Under the Yellow and Red Stars by Alex Levin
Vanished Boyhood by George Stern
The Violin by Rachel Shtibel / *A Child's Testimony* by Adam Shtibel
W Hour by Arthur Ney
We Sang in Hushed Voices by Helena Jockel

Spring's End
John Freund

THIRD PRINTING

THE AZRIELI FOUNDATION
www.azrielifoundation.org

Cover and book design by Mark Goldstein
Endpaper maps by Martin Gilbert
Cartography by Karen Van Kerkoerle

LIBRARY AND ARCHIVES CANADA CATALOGUING IN PUBLICATION

Freund, John, 1930–
    Spring's end: memoirs/ by John Freund.

(Azrieli Series of Holocaust Survivor Memoirs)
Includes bibliographical references and index.
ISBN 978-1-897470-03-9

1. Freund, John, 1930– . 2. Holocaust, Jewish (1939–1945) – Czech Republic – personal narratives. 3. Jewish children in the Holocaust – Czech Republic – Biography. 4. Holocaust survivors – Canada – Biography. I. Azrieli Foundation.
II. York University (Toronto, Ont.). Centre for Jewish Studies. III. Title.
IV. Series.

D804.196.F74 2007   940.53'18092   C2007–905441–2

PRINTED IN CANADA

The Azrieli Series of Holocaust Survivor Memoirs

Naomi Azrieli, Publisher

Sara R. Horowitz, Chair
Irving Abella
Michael Brown
Mark Webber
Kalman Weiser

Senior Editor for this volume: Sara R. Horowitz
Tamarah Feder, Managing Editor & Program Manager (2005–2008)

Maps by Sir Martin Gilbert

Contents

Series Preface:
In their own words. . .

The Azrieli Foundation – York University Holocaust Survivor Memoirs Publishing Program (Canada) was established to preserve and share the written memoirs of those who survived the twentieth century Nazi genocide of the Jews of Europe and who later made their way to Canada. The Program is guided by the conviction that each survivor of the Holocaust has a remarkable story to tell, and that such stories have an important role in education about tolerance and diversity.

Millions of individual stories are lost to us forever. The murdered Jews of Europe, of course, did not leave behind memoirs of their final days. By preserving the stories that survivors have written, and making them accessible to a broad public, the Program aims to sustain the memory of all those who perished at the hands of hatred, abetted by indifference and apathy. The personal accounts of those who survived against all odds are as different as the people who wrote them, but all demonstrate the courage, strength, wit and luck that it took to face and outlive terrible adversity. More than half a century later, the diversity of stories allows readers to put a face on what was lost, and to grasp the enormity of what happened to six million Jews – one story at a time. The memoirs are also moving tributes to people – strangers and friends – who risked their lives to help others, and who, through acts of kindness and decency in the darkest of moments, frequently helped the persecuted maintain faith in humanity and courage to endure. The accounts of how these survivors went on to build new lives in Canada after the war offers inspiration to all, as does their desire to share their experiences so that new generations can learn from them.

The Program seeks to collect, archive, edit and publish these distinctive historical records from fellow Canadians, and make them easily and freely accessible through Canadian libraries, Holocaust memorial organizations and online at The Azrieli Foundation website. The York University Centre for Jewish Studies has provided scholarly assistance and guidance in the editing and preparation of these memoirs for publication. The manuscripts as originally submitted are preserved in the Clara Thomas Archives and Special Collections at York University, and are available for review by interested scholars. These memoirs are published under the imprint The Azrieli Series of Holocaust Survivor Memoirs.

∽

The Azrieli Foundation – York University Holocaust Survivor Memoirs Publishing Program gratefully acknowledges the many people who assisted in the preparation of this series for publication. Special thanks go to Jody Spiegel, Executive Coordinator of the Azrieli Foundation. For their invaluable contributions in editing, fact-checking and proofreading the manuscripts, the Program is grateful to Todd Biderman, Helen Binik, Tali Boritz, Mark Celinscak, Mark Clamen, Jordana DeBloeme, Andrea Geddes-Poole, Valerie Hébert, Joe Hodes, Tomaz Jardim, Irena Kohn, Tatjana Lichtenstein, Carson Phillips, Randall Schnoor, Tatyana Shestakov, and Mia Spiro. For their help and support in numerous ways, the Program would like to thank Susan Alper, Mary Arvanitakis, Howard Aster, Miriam Beckerman, François Blanc, Sheila Fischman, Esther Goldberg, Agripino Monteiro, Stan Morantz (Andora Graphics), Ariel Pulver, Michael Quddus, Henia Reinhartz, Nochem Reinhartz, Mark Veldhoven and Don Winkler.

About the Glossary

The following memoir contains a number of terms, concepts and historical references that may be unfamiliar to the reader. For information on major organizations; significant historical events and people; geographical locations; religious and cultural terms; and foreign-language words and expressions that will help give context and background to the events described in the text, please see the glossary beginning on page 79.

Introduction

John Freund's memoir, *Spring's End*, recounts John's life from early childhood in a close and loving family, through the harrowing experiences that took him to Theresienstadt, to the Czech Family Camp in Auschwitz, through death marches, to liberation and rehabilitation and, finally, to sanctuary and a new life in Canada. It is a story of survival, a story of the life of a young man who witnessed much evil and the loss of everything he held dear. It is also a story of hope and regeneration, of the will to live and to honour his parents and his upbringing by becoming educated, learning a profession, raising a family and being a proud citizen in a new land.

John Freund was born in 1930 into an educated, established family in České Budějovice, located about one hundred miles south of Prague, in the southern part of Bohemia, a province of Czechoslovakia. At the time of John's birth, České Budějovice was a prosperous town of about 50,000 residents, including a Jewish community of 1,138. John's father, Gustav, was a well-regarded and devoted pediatrician. His family was, as John put it, "well-rooted" in České Budějovice; for generations they had been judges, teachers and men of business. John's mother, Erna, had grown up in the Czech town of Pisek and had received an exemplary education; she instilled in her two sons, John and Karel, a love of literature and music. The extended family on both sides – musicians, scientists, publishers, bankers and senior civil servants – lived in Vienna and Prague.

For John, life before the war was filled with the joys of childhood – soccer, school and the mischievous behaviour of little boys. Summers were spent at a farm in a nearby village enjoying the freedoms of country life – swimming, bicycling and hiking in the forests. In his early years in school, John was the only Jewish child although, as he writes, "I was not very aware that, because I was Jewish, I was different from others." John's family, like many, identified itself as "strongly Czech" although his grandfather, Alexander Freund, insisted that his grandchildren receive a Jewish religious education. The effort to integrate a religious, cultural and national identity for the Freund family – and other Czech Jews – was not easy. John writes of his grandfather's sentiments in 1927 that although it had been "recommended that he become baptized to improve his career, he refused to give up his Jewish religion." It was a time when Jews were accepted into professions and into society as long as they stopped being Jews. Many chose this option to further their position and their security in life; many chose to continue to live as Jews.

Czechoslovakia was created as a nation in 1918 at the end of World War I, carved out of the collapse of the Austro-Hungarian Empire. Its first president, Tomáš Masaryk, created a democratic constitution and society, but with the worldwide economic collapse in 1929, the Czech minorities – Ruthenes, Slovaks, Hungarians, and the German-speaking people of the Sudetenland – pressed for greater autonomy. Nazi Germany exploited this instability to further its territorial ambitions. In March 1938, Germany annexed its neighbour, Austria; in October 1938, with the approval of Britain and France, the Germans marched into the Sudetenland area of Czechoslovakia. Five months later, Germany annexed the Czech provinces of Bohemia and Moravia, including the Czech capital, Prague, and John Freund's hometown of České Budějovice.

Under German occupation, the lives of the Jews of České Budějovice changed dramatically. Public facilities, restaurants, cinemas and, most importantly for John, schools, once open to all, were immediately closed to Jews by German decree. John writes, "The pessimists thought one to two years and all would be back to normal; the optimists talked of weeks. It took six years and, for us at least, things never got back to normal." John was nine years old.

Excluded from the general community, John and his Jewish friends found companionship and solidarity among their own. Trying to maintain a normal life, Jewish families set up schools in private homes and organized youth groups, believing that the worst was over. The community's children spent the summers of 1940 and 1941 on a narrow strip along the Vltava River, which Jews were allowed to use for swimming and soccer and John's favourite, ping-pong. John and his young friends started a magazine, *Klepy* (Gossip), hand-typed and illustrated with stories, art, jokes and incidents; only one copy of each issue was printed and carefully passed around.[1] At a time when the Jews of Poland were being concentrated in Polish ghettos under increasingly grim conditions, John and his mates "cherished each day and prayed that the summer of 1941 would never end. Except for a handful of us, it was the last summer." John was eleven.

On April 18, 1942, a transport of 909 Jews from České Budějovice, including Gustav and Erna Freund and their sons Karel and John, was taken to the former Czech garrison town of Terezín, run by the Germans as a ghetto and transit camp and known in German as Theresienstadt. During the month of April 1942, five transports from Prague and the regions nearby reached Theresienstadt with a total of 4,832 Jews. At that time, the population of the ghetto of Theresienstadt was 12,986, all from Bohemia and Moravia. In its three and a half years of operation, nearly 140,000 people passed through Theresienstadt: Jews from Bohemia and Moravia, Germany, Austria, Holland, Denmark and Slovakia.

With the masses of people being deported into Theresienstadt,

---

1   The originals are held at the Jewish Museum in Prague / Židovské muzeum v Praze.

conditions in the ghetto were grim; the inhabitants experienced overcrowding, malnutrition, disease and the omnipresent fear of the dreaded and continual deportations. However, at the end of 1942, in order to strengthen the deception that the Jews were living well in Theresienstadt before being resettled "in the East" and to counter growing concerns about their well-being, the Germans allowed inmates to engage in cultural activities. A town of pretense, the concerts, theatre, art and poetry created the façade of a "model camp" that was to be part of the German propaganda machine. In September 1944, the Nazis ordered one of the inmates, Kurt Gerron, a distinguished pre-war German-Jewish filmmaker, to make a propaganda film, *The Führer Gives the Jews a City*, to maintain the fiction that Jews were being treated well. The film was never shown during the war as too many of the scenes failed to convey the positive impressions the Nazis wanted.

We know now that the hundreds of thousands of Jews in Western and Central Europe who were taken from their homes and transit camps were deported to their deaths in Auschwitz, Chelmno, Treblinka, Sobibor, Belzec and Maly Trostinets.

For Jewish prisoners at Theresienstadt, these cultural activities became, as the chronicler Zdeněk Lederer writes in his landmark study, *Ghetto Theresienstadt*, "the focal point of artistic achievement and a weapon of spiritual and intellectual resistance by the Jews." It was this expression of creativity that set life at Theresienstadt apart from other camps and ghettos. Their art and their creation of it is a testament to the resistance of evil that happened on every level and in every place. During the year and a half that John was imprisoned in Theresienstadt, he was able to take advantage of these intellectual activities. He wrote poems for the weekly news magazine, attended talks by teachers and put on plays. He even had his bar mitzvah in Theresienstadt, taught by his rabbi from České Budějovice. A normal life amid the deprivations of imprisonment was continually sought – and shakily established.

In December 1943, the Freund family was deported from Theresienstadt. None of the deportees knew where they were being sent, or what had happened to those who had been deported previously. They were told only that they were being sent "to the East." Their journey took two days crammed and locked into a cattle car. They arrived and were told that they had come to a place called Auschwitz. John writes, "It seemed like another planet." It was. John was thirteen.

The Jews who came from Theresienstadt had a different reception from the hundreds of thousands of other Jews who were deported to Auschwitz between the summer of 1942 and November 1944. Rather than the normal routine of facing immediate *Selektion* after disembarking from the train – the separation of those who were considered able-bodied and therefore capable of work, from the elderly, the infirm and the very young with their mothers to be murdered – the Jews from Theresienstadt were allowed to remain together as families. They were taken to Camp B-IIb in the Birkenau section of Auschwitz, which became known as the Czech Family Camp.

The Czech Family Camp had been established at Auschwitz with the arrival of 5,006 Jews from Theresienstadt on September 8, 1943. These Jewish prisoners were kept together and had slightly better conditions than elsewhere in Birkenau. Again, as with Theresienstadt, this was intended by the Nazis as a way to counteract news of the mass murder of Jews that was starting to trickle out to the West. To maintain the lie that they had only been "resettled" in the East, these Czech prisoners were encouraged to write postcards to members of their families still in Czechoslovakia. Of those in the Czech Family Camp who had been there since September, 1,000 died during the winter. Physicians and pairs of twins forced to undergo medical experiments were removed from the group. The rest were killed in the gas chambers on March 7, 1944, six months after their arrival.

John Freund and his family arrived in the second group to inhabit the Czech Family Camp, arriving in Auschwitz on December 16, 1943. Six months later, on July 2, 1944, with approximately 10,000 Jews in the Czech Family Camp, 3,080 were chosen – 2,000 women, 1,000 men, all of whom were sent to concentration camps in Germany, and eighty younger boys sent for vocational training. In this selection, John was among the younger boys, and his brother and father among the men. Erna Freund was among the 3,000 women and children taken to the gas chambers on July 10.

A Slovak Jewish prisoner, Rudolf Vrba, who had been a registrar in Birkenau, was able to move freely between the Czech Family Camp and other areas of Birkenau. In March 1944, he passed on messages from the resistance movement in Auschwitz to the effect that the *Sonderkommando*, those whose job it was to remove the bodies from the gas chambers, were prepared to resist on March 7 if the Czech Jews would begin the resistance. Rudolf Vrba asked Fredy Hirsch, whom John Freund knew well, to signal the resistance. Fredy Hirsch had been working with the young children of the Czech Family Camp and could not bear the thought of what would happen. He committed suicide on March 6. The resistance at the gas chambers did not bring about the planned effect, although there was some individual fighting. The Czech Jews entered the gas chambers singing the Czech national anthem and "Hatikvah" (Hope), now the national anthem of Israel.

Rudolf Vrba and the Resistance knew that those who had arrived in December would be killed in six months, as those who had come in September had been murdered in March. He and his fellow Slovak Jew, Alfred Weztler, escaped from Auschwitz on April 7 with the intention of alerting the world that the so-called "unknown destination in the East" was a killing centre, and that those in the Czech Family Camp were imminently going to be killed. Their report, which reached the West, became known as the Auschwitz Report. It was later substantiated by another Slovak Jew, Arnošt Rosin, and a Polish Jew, Czesław Mordowicz, both of whom escaped in May, reporting that the Hungarian Jews were at that very moment being deported to their deaths in Auschwitz. These four reports were combined and constituted the first eyewitness accounts to reach the West of the nature and purpose of Auschwitz. The report reached the West in June 1944, as the Normandy landings were taking place and Germany faced military challenges from both East and West. The report was not able to stop the gassings of the Czech Family Camp or the tens of thousands of Jews who were being deported from the Hungarian provinces, but it was a major factor in ending the deportations from Budapest.

John Freund was able to survive in Auschwitz until January 1945 when the Nazis evacuated the camp. Forced to move west ahead of the Soviet army, John was among thousands of others taken on a death march from January until April when he was liberated by American troops.

As word of the mass murder of Jews leaked to the outside world during World War II, two major deception plans were imposed by the Nazis to lull the non-Jewish world into believing the "rumours" were not correct, and to lull Europe's Jews into peacefully boarding the deportation trains that would, in the end, take them to their deaths. These two deceptions, Theresienstadt and the Czech Family Camp in Birkenau, have their place in the history of the Holocaust. John Freund's memoir describes his experiences in these two camps in rich detail.

John's memoir also illuminates the state of post-war Czechoslovakia and gives us insight into the choices people faced at that time. After his liberation, John went to Prague to resume his studies and to try to find and reconnect with friends who had survived. With the political instability of Czechoslovakia and Stalin's aspirations to dominate it, John looked for an opportunity to leave.

On March 12, 1948, John left Prague in a group of thirty children under the age of eighteen to make a new life in Canada; they were among the 16,000 survivors who came to Canada in the first five years after the war. He married a Czech Jewish girl who, along with her parents, had found asylum in Canada before the war, one family among the 6,000 German, Austrian and Czech Jews who came to Canada between 1933 and 1938. Canada's contribution to the plight of refugees, both before the war and after, was important. The story of his second life, in Canada, is a testament to a spirit that although hurt, could not be crushed, rising above human depravity to create a robust life that included a loving wife, children and a career.

John's passion for music, art, poetry and life have flourished in spite of the cruelties he witnessed and suffered as a boy. But it was the childhood and his home life that influenced him after the war. The love that so many survivors had felt in their homes before the war and the Jewish education they had received helped them to return to their roots after liberation, to continue the education of which they had been so cruelly deprived during the years of terror and war, and to rebuild the families and the homes they had lost. *Spring's End* is the story of the strength of the human spirit to survive and the need of the human spirit to seek peace and find happiness in life.

Esther Goldberg
London, Ontario
August 2007

SOURCES

Czech, Danuta. *Auschwitz Chronicle, 1939–1945.* London: I.B. Taurus & Co., 1990.

"České Budějovice," *Encyclopedia Judaica*, Jerusalem: Keter Publishing House, 1972.

Gilbert, Martin. *Atlas of the Holocaust.* London: Routledge, 2002.

Gilbert, Martin. *Auschwitz and the Allies.* London: Pimlico, 2001.

Gilbert, Martin. *The European Powers, 1900–1946.* London: Phoenix, 2002.

Gilbert, Martin. *The History of the Twentieth Century*, Vol. 1, 1900–1933. London: HarperCollins, 1997.

Goldberg, Esther. *Holocaust Memoir Digest*, Vol. 1. London: Vallentine Mitchell, 2004.

Lederer, Zdeněk . *Ghetto Theresienstadt.* New York: Fertig, 1983.

John Freund's distinctive poetic writing style paints vivid memories of a child-like innocence with the intensity those memories still carry for him as an adult. The original manuscript, available for scholarly consultation at York University's Clara Thomas and Special Collection Archives, was written over a period of years. That original text contains recurring vignettes of certain experiences, each version told as though John were standing at a different angle, describing what it was he saw in the landscape of his memory. The memoir you read here was edited to minimize confusion that might be inherent in those repetitive anecdotes and to help reveal a clear narrative. However, those original repetitions and other descriptions of seemingly innocuous events that trigger a flood of memories reveal how the events of John Freund's life are replayed, willingly or not. This is a testament that liberation from concentration camps did not necessarily bring about the end of the suffering or mourning or anger. The determined spirits and hopeful imaginations of many survivors like John lived alongside their haunted memories to recreate a semblance of what was stolen.

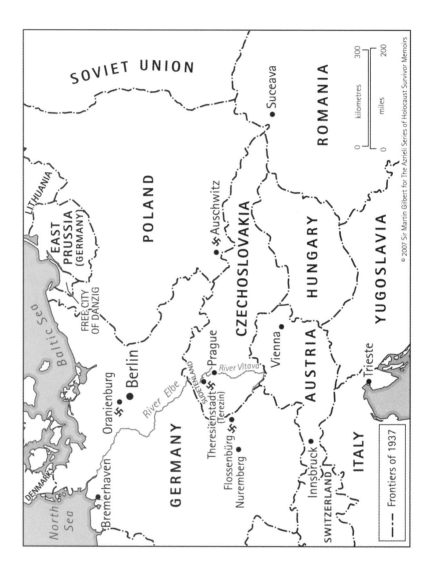

SOVIET UNION

ROMANIA

Suceava

LITHUANIA

EAST
PRUSSIA
(GERMANY)

POLAND

✡Auschwitz

CZECHOSLOVAKIA

HUNGARY

FREE CITY
OF DANZIG

Baltic Sea

YUGOSLAVIA

Berlin

Oranienburg

River Elbe

Prague

River Vltava

Vienna

AUSTRIA

Trieste

North
Sea

DENMARK

Bremerhaven

GERMANY

SUDETENLAND

Theresienstadt
(Terezin)

Flossenbürg

Nuremberg

Innsbruck

SWITZERLAND

ITALY

kilometres

miles

300

200

0

0

© 2007 Sir Martin Gilbert for The Azrieli Series of Holocaust Survivor Memoirs

--- Frontiers of 1937

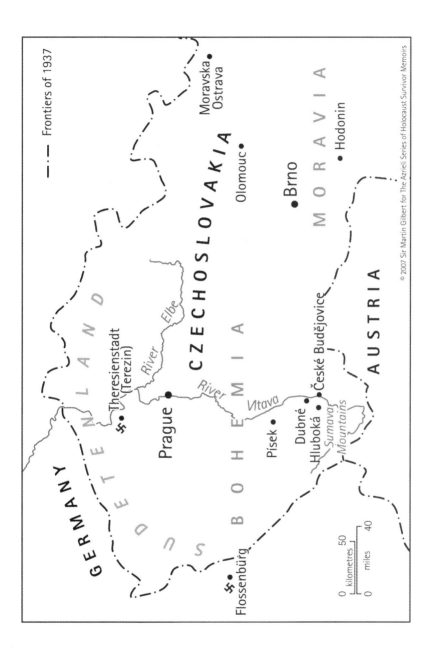

Frontiers of 1937

GERMANY

SUDETENLAND

BOHEMIA

CZECHOSLOVAKIA

MORAVIA

AUSTRIA

Flossenbürg ☪

Theresienstadt
(Terezin) ☪

Prague •

Písek •

Dubné •

Hluboká •

České Budějovice •

Šumava
Mountains

River Elbe

River Vltava

Olomouc •

• Brno

Moravska
Ostrava •

• Hodonin

0 kilometres 50

0 miles 40

© 2007 Sir Martin Gilbert for The Azrieli Series of Holocaust Survivor Memoirs

Even as a young boy, I knew I wanted to write. When I was thirteen, I wrote the poem below while in the Terezín Ghetto:

It's already five years
Since into peace marched a devil.
Death has moved from house to house;
War brought terrible times.
Mothers and daughters light candles
Remembering those beloved
Whom they will never see again.

Let me start my story with my childhood, a time of peace, before the entrance of the Devil in 1939.

Chapter One

My childhood was full of joy and adventure and, occasionally, pain. My family, the Freunds, consisted of my father, Gustav, my mother, Erna, my older brother, Karel, and me.[1] We lived in a town called České Budějovice, which was located at the junction of two rivers, the Vltava (Moldau) and the Malše, in southern Bohemia. Our town of 50,000 inhabitants was 160 kilometres south of the beautiful city of Prague, the capital of Czechoslovakia.

As a small child, I loved splashing around in the water in the summer and playing in the snow in winter. When I was older, I learned to swim and skate. We did a lot of things together as a family. My father had a car, which was rare in the early 1930s, and on Sundays, we drove out of town to the nearby mountain range of Šumava. There, we picnicked and climbed the mountain. Sometimes, other families would join us, which was always a lot of fun.

We spent summers in a tiny village near Šumava, just thirty-two kilometres from Budějovice. Father was a pediatrician and was not

---

1 At birth, I was given the name Hanus, which I later disliked, so when I was five, it was changed to Jan.

able to come with us as he had to work. We would take walks in the forest and swim in small ponds. I loved to sit by a large tree along the roadside, catching butterflies with my net.

Budějovice was an old town, founded in the Middle Ages by the Bohemian King Ottokar II. Budějovice was sometimes referred to by its German name, "Budweiss." Beer had been brewed in our town since the fourteenth century, though it was not until much later that a brewery began to export beer under the name "Budweisser." In earlier times, Budějovice had to protect itself from invaders. An old, crumbling wall remained from this time, along with a tall, black tower in the centre of the town. All the boys living in Budějovice would show their courage by climbing to the top of the Black Tower on its narrow, winding staircase, in complete darkness. The Black Tower held a "torture doll." Although I never saw the doll, the story circulated that during the Middle Ages, prisoners were thrown inside the larger-than-life figure. It had nails on the inside and the metal floor was said to be heated until it was red hot. No one came out alive. Every child growing up in Budějovice knew about the torture doll. It made little difference that it had not been used since the Middle Ages. Who knew when it might be used again?

My family lived in an apartment building near the town centre. The building was owned by a wealthy butcher, Mr. Kocer, and his wife. They had become rich during World War I. They operated their butcher shop on the street level of Jírovcova Street No. 11, which was our address from the time of my birth in 1930 until we were forced out in April 1942. Our apartment was large. It had its own little staircase leading to it from the main staircase. My brother and I slept and played in the children's room.

My brother, Karel, was three years older than I and was a difficult child. He would always take things from me and hit and kick me. We were always fighting. I was considered the good little boy and he the bad one. When I was seven years old, I almost killed Karel. Our apartment building had a small yard with several garages and the yard was enclosed by a tall gate. One day, my brother closed the gate behind me, locking me in the yard. I pleaded with him to let me out, but he just laughed. So I took a nearby rock and threw it over the gate. It was a direct hit. Karel got a big gash on his head and began bleeding badly. He was rushed to the hospital and his cut was stitched up. I was in big trouble. I got a long lecture and the town rabbi, Dr. Ferda, was brought in to counsel me on my misdeed, asking me questions like, "What if a mother had been pushing her buggy and your rock had hit the baby...?"

As you can see, my brother and I were quite mischievous. In fact, my parents were constantly under threat of being thrown out of the apartment because of us. Not surprisingly, we attracted other rowdy boys. One day, the noise inside our apartment rose so high that our landlady, Mrs. Kocer, came to knock on our door. No one dared to go and open it! Eventually, she broke through the front door, only to find a group of boys in the apartment, sitting on wardrobes and hiding in corners. I was hiding in the closet, and she chased me around our beautiful dining-room table with a nasty broom. When she caught me, she really let me have it!

My parents were relatively calm people, Mother especially. She was very small and very pretty. I loved going shopping with her to the delicatessen stores in the big square. I would always end up with a fresh roll and thinly sliced hot dog.

MY MOTHER AND HER FAMILY

Mother was born and grew up in a small Czech town named Pisek. She went only to Czech schools and disliked it when people around her spoke German.[2] Her maiden name was Jung. The Jungs were

---

2 National identity in interwar Czechoslovakia was a highly contentious issue. The areas of Bohemia and Moravia had a combined German population of three mil-

progressive people: Uncle Leopold, my mother's brother, was sent to law school, and my mother and her sister finished high school. My mother was very proud of her matriculation from a *Gymnasium* (high school).

Mother liked to read and discuss books with her friends, and she frequently went to the library. She seemed a sad person, often staring into the distance. I think she missed her brother and sister, with whom she was very close. Her brother, Leopold (Poldi), lived in Prague and had an important government position in the revenue department. He was married to Manja, a round-faced, pleasant person, and they had two daughters.

My mother was closest with her sister, Anna (nicknamed Anda), who lived in Innsbruck, Austria. The two sisters were always corresponding. Anda was a beautiful girl. She met her husband, Robert Fleck, on a train sometime around 1917. He was tall and handsome and wore an Austrian uniform, just like Anda's father had. They were young and fell in love. I don't know how religiously active my Jung grandparents were, but it hurt them that Anda married out of the Jewish faith. However, Anda and Robert had a wonderful marriage.

Both Mother and Anda were very good pianists. I remember Mother playing Chopin waltzes; however, she maintained that Anda

---

lion. Before the founding of Czechoslovakia in 1918, the region was part of the Austro-Hungarian Empire. Therefore, the Jews of Czechoslovakia were highly westernized and acculturated as they had achieved emancipation in 1867 under the Austro-Hungarian Empire. During the interwar period, the Jews of Bohemia and Moravia were forced to choose between the two dominant cultures of the region – German and Czech. The majority chose the German high culture over Czech culture from a linguistic standpoint by sending their children to German-language schools. However, this situation was far from simple. See Ezra Mendelsohn, *The Jews of East Central Europe Between the World Wars* (Bloomington, IN: Indiana University Press, 1987), 131–169.

was a far better pianist. My parents thought that I, too, had some talent in piano and they arranged lessons for me. One of my teachers was a lady with the Old Testament name of Mrs. Jeremiah. Twenty-five years earlier, she had been my mother's teacher. I took piano lessons for three years until 1941.

There is an interesting story about my mother's grandfather, Jacob Jung. He was a high-school teacher and taught classical languages like Latin and Hebrew. He had a terrible temper. One day, he descended upon one of his students in great anger and pulled at his ear so hard that blood started to gush out of it. There was a scandal, but Professor Jung was forgiven – until the next time. When next time came, his anger led him to take a burning desk oil lamp and hurl it at a student who was dozing off in the class. That was the end of this part of his career – there were no more classes for the professor.

One of Jacob Jung's sons was named Adolf – a decent name before the beast, Adolf Hitler, made it infamous. Our family's Adolf ran away from home when he was eleven years old and joined a local army camp as a shoeshine boy. He stayed in the army for the rest of his life. He rose through the ranks to become a major in the then-powerful Austro-Hungarian Army. This was a very high position for a Jew. He looked a little bit like the Emperor Franz Josef, the great leader of the Austro-Hungarian Empire. Adolf was my mother's father.

I remember my mother's parents as being very old. They lived in Prague. Grandpa Adolf, who still wore his major's uniform, was quite deaf. Grandmother Rosa was very elegant. I was told that she came from a very rich, aristocratic family. Grandma Rosa was not the military type. She was dark and beautiful and proud of her Spanish heritage. Her family name before her marriage was Fischoff. Both her parents died very young and so she was brought up by two wealthy uncles in a town called Suceava in Romania. Her uncles owned the most beautiful house in the town. It still stands today and in the 1970s was used as the Communist Party headquarters for the area. Rosa was attended to by servants, and her uncles insisted that she be taught properly and not spoiled. In 1890, at the age of seventeen, she married the soldier Adolf, the son of an unemployed high school teacher. She received two thousand gold coins for her dowry. Imagine!

Rosa had a sister, whose name I don't know, but her sister's daughter was Hansi Biener. Aunt Hansi came to live in Toronto in 1950. She was very eccentric, terribly snobbish and a great pianist. As a child, she travelled around the world with a group of musicians and gave concerts in Detroit and Windsor in the 1920s. Aunt Hansi was proud to tell us that a long time ago the Fischoffs had been a well-known family in Vienna as great-great-grandfather Fischoff was a famous music teacher at the Vienna Conservatory.

THE FREUNDS

My father laughed and joked a lot but, like my mother, he too seemed sad. He was a children's doctor and perhaps took on many of the worries of his young patients' mothers. He regularly visited a local café. Children were not permitted in this fancy, smoke-filled club where the men played cards, read newspapers, and discussed politics and who knows what else. Father had studied in Berlin and spoke Czech with a German accent. He was part of the German-speaking Jewish population of Czechoslovakia.

When I was a little boy, I loved being sick because it was then that my father's kindness was fully available to me. Father often spent hours with very sick children, encouraging them and giving them confidence to recover from their illnesses. He often stayed with a sick child day and night until the worst was over.

Later on in life, when I was in Terezín and he was a doctor in our living quarters, I was very proud to see him walking around in his white coat.

My father's family was rooted in Budějovice. My grandfather Alexander, whom I never knew, had been a county judge and his chambers were in the Budějovice city hall. People say he was strict and a very strange character, as he often walked around town talking to himself. He died in 1927. Grandfather Alexander's father was named Moses and he was a businessman. I know nothing more about the Freunds except that one of Moses' brothers went to England and his family may have moved to America.

I suspect that the strongest person in my family was my grandmother Hermine, who was Alexander's wife. Hermine came from the Bondy family who were rich and owned a flour mill in Prague. The only Bondy I remember was my great-grandmother Veronika, Hermine's mother. Veronika lived to be 102 years old and died in Prague in 1940. She lived there with my grandmother Hermine in an old, dirty apartment building they owned on Karlin Street. It still stands in Prague and we still own a part of it.

When I was little, I was frightened of my grandmother and great-grandmother, Hermine and Veronika. At the time, Veronika was in her nineties and was always spitting into a handkerchief. There were two other women living in their dark apartment. One of the women was their faithful maid and the other was Hermine's unmarried daughter – my Aunt Randa. Aunt Randa was an "old maid" and a strange person. I don't know much about her, except that the Freunds would talk about her only in whispers.

If Aunt Randa was strange, her sister Else was even stranger. She was never talked about when children were present. As the story goes, sometime around the 1920s, my aunt began believing in some type of supernatural power and joined an organization that promoted such beliefs. She stopped looking after herself, began overeating and drinking a lot, and kept bad company. A man appeared in her life – some small-time crook. To the disgust of her family, she went to live with him in Berlin. He was only interested in her money, not in her. This sad story ends with her getting pregnant and dying in childbirth.

My father had a third sister, Anna, who was always immaculately clean, confident and full of élan. She was married to a strict, self-assured man named Maximilian Weiss. The Weisses lived in Prague in a beautiful, large apartment building that was so modern it had an elevator. You would catch the elevator in the apartment and it would open in the building lobby. At that time there were only a few such buildings in the world. Uncle Max was a brilliant man. He was a professor at a well-known business academy and later became the director and manager of the large Union Bank. It was very rare for a Jew to have such an important position. Uncle Max came from a humble, observant family, but he did not pass much religion on to his children.

The Weisses were upper class and did not like visiting their doctor brother, Gustl, in Budějovice, with his "bluestocking" wife and their two bratty sons.[3] Even so, the Weisses were admirable. They had three children: Willie, Hans and Marianne.

My father's youngest brother, Ernst, his wife, Mitzi, and their daughter, Eva, left Europe in 1939, just in time to avoid the terrible troubles the war brought. They settled in New York and changed their family name to Forgan.[4]

My father's oldest brother, Franz, who made a living as a soap salesman, was always full of jokes and talked very loudly. Franz, his wife, Irma, and their two children, Freddie and Fanci, lived in Budějovice.

SCHOOL DAYS

My school days started in Grade 1, in an old, four-storey building just a couple of blocks away from our home. If I looked from my window across the blacksmith's yard, I could see the red-brick school. It smelled of urine from the poorly kept bathrooms. We had narrow wooden benches, three boys to a bench, with a row of desk tops.

---

3 This is a derogatory term used to refer to intellectual or literary women.

4 Eva, who was my age, married a very nice man, Edgar Merkel.

My first day of school was long and frightening, but the teacher was a nice lady who ended up teaching me the next year, too. Her husband was my teacher for Grades 3 and 4. On the first day of school, the principal came into our class. He was tall with grey hair, and looked like somebody's old grandfather. It was an all-boys school – all the schools were divided by gender at this time. The boys were mainly from poor families and were full of pranks. I was the only Jewish boy in the class. I made good friends with a boy named Zdeněk Švec, whose father was a superintendent at a nearby school. We spent a lot of time together. We loved walking through the dark corridors of the school where Zdeněk 's father worked at night. Rope-driven elevators, which were just platforms, were prohibited to us. However, sometimes we got brave and rode them between floors. Zdeněk 's parents were decent, hard-working people. They lived in the school and their combined living-room/kitchen was always warm and smelled of baking. Zdeněk and I played cards.

As a child, I was not aware that I was different from others because I was Jewish. My family observed the Jewish holidays. I remember our Passover seders, when we sat around our round dining-room table and Father read Hebrew prayers from a black book. At Chanukah, we lit candles, sang Maóz Tsur (Rock of Ages), and received presents. I felt a special family warmth during these celebrations.

As both grandfathers were public servants, my parents came from homes that were part of the broader Czech community, far away from the Jewish ghettos of earlier days. Grandfather Freund, a judge, saw to it that his children attended religious school, but he was not particularly observant. However, when it was recommended that he become baptized to improve his career, he refused to give up his Jewish religion.

Even though my grandparents were not persecuted, they knew they were considered "different." Past experiences of oppression were not too distant from their memories. When my mother's sister, Aunt Anda, married a Christian in Innsbruck, it saddened my grandparents, but they did not attempt to interfere. Aunt Anda was baptized in order to marry her beloved Robert, who was a Catholic, but her parents never learned of this. Some of my friends were Jewish, but most were not. This was, of course, before the Nazi invasion and the terrible hatred it stirred up.

In my early school years, from 1936 to 1939, we felt strongly Czech. Once, the president of the Republic, Mr. Beneš, visited Budějovice and all the children lined up along the streets waving the red, white and blue flag of the country. We sang the Czech national anthem, "Where Is My Land."

Our great hero was Tomáš G. Masaryk, the founder of the Czechoslovak Republic in 1918. Masaryk was the son of a poor coachman. When he grew up, he became a famous professor. He loved learning, and justice was important to him. He was the president of Czechoslovakia from 1918 (after the collapse of the Austrian Empire, following World War I) to 1935. Pictures of him riding a horse were in our textbooks and hung on school walls.

Masaryk was a great Czech nationalist who believed, first and foremost, in truth. His motto was "Pravda Zvítězí" (Truth Will Prevail). While a professor, Masaryk defended a Jewish peasant, Leopold Hilsner. This man was falsely accused of murdering a Christian child by superstitious Christians who believed blood was needed to bake matzoh for Passover. Masaryk was a devout Christian and he stood up against injustice. He successfully defended Hilsner by proving to the judge and country that the old superstition was a lie.

T.G.M., as Masaryk was known, had a favourite song, "Ach Synku." The verses translate as:

"Hey Sonny, did you work today? Did you plough the field?"
"No, I did not, Papa, my plough has broken down."
"If it has broken down, then repair it, Sonny; learn to be reliant."

It was during those idealistic days that my parents married and my brother and I were born. The idea of a democratic republic, with a wise and just president, was beautiful. Unfortunately, there were economic problems in Czechoslovakia, as there were throughout the world. There was unemployment and poverty, and Czechoslovakia was a small country that neighboured the aggressive and powerful Germany.

Starting in Grade 1, I attended religious classes twice a week. Rabbi Ferda came to our school and taught all the Jewish children together for two one-hour sessions. Rabbi Ferda taught us from a book called *Sinai*. It had the old stories and pictures of the far-away land called Palestine. Rabbi Ferda was happy with Czechoslovakia and Tomáš G. Masaryk, but he did not believe our peaceful situation would last. When Tomáš Masaryk died in 1937, we all wept. Two years later, Hitler's armies made their way into Czechoslovakia, bringing along with them his overwhelming hatred of the Jews.

Like many other families, we had household help. I remember only two of our helpers – Maria and Karla. Maria was tall, slim and very nice. She got mixed up with a soldier and had a baby. Maria sent the baby to live with her parents and came back to work for us. Karla had a big bosom and I remember she often had her breasts uncovered. Maybe that's why she did not stay with us for long.

Of all the seasons, I loved spring the best. I would watch the thick ice on our kitchen window slowly melt and the pretty ice designs disappear. When spring arrived, we would open the windows wide to let in the wonderful fresh air. The large trees in the private garden under our windows produced blossoms with a heavenly aroma. Springtime meant that my mother and I would go to buy me a new pair of shoes. Instead of the long stockings I wore all winter, I got to wear short socks. I felt like a bird that had just learned to fly.

Like all the boys in my neighbourhood, I loved to play soccer. I would always dribble the ball, passing it to my teammates or taking shots at the goal. When I was seven years old, my favourite soccer team, Slavia Praha, won the European Cup. Plánička, the slim, handsome goalie, saved many goals with the most spectacular action: he would toss himself six metres in the air to keep the ball out of his net.

In the last minute of the game, the star forward of Slavia shot the ball into the net of the startled opposing team and we won! I was so excited. The story was reported all over the radio and I could not stop talking about it. I dreamed of becoming a famous sportsman but my success was slow in coming.

The first sport I succeeded in was not soccer, but ping-pong. I played at the municipal swimming area in Budějovice at the edge of town, along the Vltava River. It had two fairly large swimming pools, a shallow one for non-swimmers and one that was over two metres deep. The daring would swim in the fast-flowing river, but I stayed far away from it. Along the two pools, there was a nicely landscaped area for small children and wooden planks for sunbathers. In one corner there was a collection of small buildings where you could buy refreshments and play ping-pong. I spent a lot of time improving my game. These were the happy summer days of 1938. Though the grownups were disturbed whenever they listened to the radio, nothing bothered me that summer.

One of my favourite pastimes was walking around the town. There was an old man on the bank of the Malše River who made rope with a spinning wheel. I would watch him for hours. Further along the river, there was an ice cutter. He would cut large blocks of ice from the frozen river and lift them out with a small crane into his truck.

In my first year at school, I was chosen to recite a poem in front of the school. I borrowed a black suit with long pants and a top hat for this special performance. Even then, I hated facing any type of audience. My parents were proud, however, and the evening went off quite well.

Money was never discussed in our family. I suppose that as a doctor, my father earned a decent wage; however, I always picture him as struggling to help others. He saved the lives of many children. Whenever summoned, even late at night, he would get up and report to the call. Once, while en route to an out-of-town call in the middle of the night, he was stopped, robbed and hit on the head. It was not too serious and he made it back home on his own. After that, my mother went with him on night calls.

One day, while shopping with Mother, we found a ten-koruna bill, which at the time was worth quite a bit. Mother was so thrilled that she took us all to the best pastry shop in town for chocolate éclairs and "Indians," chocolate pyramids with cream in the middle.

One Sunday, when I was about eight, we were joined on our usual outing by Dr. Hugo Adler, an old school friend of my father's. Dr. Adler brought his wife and their two kids. Their son, Fritz, was slightly younger than me and his sister, Hana, was four. Hana was a nuisance, always getting lost in the woods or chasing squirrels. But Fritz had so many interesting things to talk about. By the time our walk was over, I was captivated and we arranged to meet again soon. So began my friendship with "Fricek," Fritz Adler. We would go tobogganing and skating. He was daring and tried everything. One day, while an additional floor was being added to our apartment building, Fricek decided to climb up the scaffolding that stood on the outer wall of the building. His fingers got stuck in some metal parts and he hung there, screaming. He was rushed to hospital. Fortunately, the damage was not so great.

Fricek and his family lived in one large room with only a small kitchen. We were frequently together and I was envious of his courage and his constant flow of ideas. He dreamed of being everything from a fireman to a pilot. When Fricek got sick and I could not visit, I felt like an orphan. His little sister, Hana, was obsessed with the desire to own a pony. She fought so hard that her kind father gave in and bought her one. She then forgot about people and lived only for the cute horse.

After a year's stay in Budějovice, the Adlers moved to distant and mysterious Norway, a land where night lasts half the year and day, the other half. My only memento of Fricek was his signature on a piece of paper. I would look at it often and wonder where he was. We would meet again later, after the war.

Another of my favourite pastimes was riding the trains or just watching them. Budějovice was an important link between Austria and Prague, so many trains passed through our town. I would stand for hours on top of a bridge. From the bridge, I could see the trains coming and leaving the station. Every train – fast, slow, freight or passenger – was a thrill. I also loved travelling by train. When we visited our grandparents in Prague, we would take the express train that sped on the rails over rivers and valleys, through tunnels and towns. During these trips, I would not move from the window for the entirety of the trip – three solid hours.

One such trip to Prague happened under bad circumstances. My mother suffered from stomach problems and went to Prague for an operation to remove part of her stomach. While in Prague, I stayed with my father's brother Ernst. His apartment was nice and on a high floor. At night, I would look out the windows at the neon lights of the big city. Ernst and his wife, Mitzi, had a daughter, Eva. She was pushy but still a nice girl. Uncle Ernst was a newspaper publisher, but when the Germans came he was kicked out of his job. Bitter and upset, he applied for papers to go to America. Soon after my visit, they left for New York. How smart they were to have the foresight to leave rotting Europe!

One day, I think in the fall, my brother and I went for a walk along a narrow river. We were quite a distance from home. The bright sky slowly darkened, followed by a heavy downpour and thunder. I can still remember feeling uneasy, for no particular reason – a premonition. We ran home, wet right through. The mood at home was thick with tension. That evening my parents listened to the radio. Several friends came over and their talk was serious. Words like "war," "Hitler," "Jew," came through frequently in the conversation. The innocence of my childhood came to an end.

Chapter Two

I was nine years old in 1939 when the German army rolled across the Austrian border into our town. It was a grim day. The scenery was full of armoured trucks, tanks, soldiers in dark green uniforms and the occasional low-flying airplane. With them, the Germans brought their dreadful Nazi ideology. They were led by their leader, Adolf Hitler, perhaps the greatest criminal political leader of all time.

When the Germans came, most people stayed indoors, but there were some who welcomed them. These were people who hated the Jews. These people were envious of those with more than they and now it was their turn to show their true colours. Nobody knew what would happen. The war had not yet started; the Czech army was ordered not to resist the invaders. The Germans took over quickly and people were arrested on the first day of the invasion. Soon, orders began appearing on bulletin boards and in newspapers.

We Jews were hit the hardest. Signs that read "Jews not permitted" appeared in cinemas, coffee houses, streetcars, public buildings, public parks and elsewhere. Schools were ordered not to allow us in and public swimming areas became prohibited to us. Once, as I walked near my home alone, I noticed my Grade 3 teacher across the street. He crossed toward me and, as we passed, he shook my hand

and quickly said, "Be brave." He took a great risk, as even talking to a Jew was regarded as a crime.

Discussion among the adults at home was often in German – perhaps so that we children could not understand. At night, we would listen to the news from England on our shortwave radio, as Czech radio was now in the hands of the Germans. At this time, there were pessimists and there were optimists. The pessimists thought that in one to two years all would be back to normal, while the optimists thought weeks. In the end, the war lasted six years and, for us, things never got back to normal.

I could no longer play with my non-Jewish friends. My friendship with Zdeněk and other non-Jewish boys came to an end. There were about three hundred Jewish families in town, and I did not know many of them. Some were professionals like us – doctors and lawyers. Others were small storekeepers and several were wealthy manufacturers. I became good friends with a group of four boys who were all my age. In our group, there were two Rudis, one Henry, one Paul and me. Before the war, Henry and one of the Rudis were rich. The other Rudi and Paul were poor. After the Germans took everything from us, we were all poor. We were required to wear a yellow Star of David on our outer garments, over our lapels. Our parents warned us to stay away from certain parts of town where it was known that there were hooligans and Nazis. I do not think that we were subjected to too much abuse at that time. Did all this drive us to despair? No way. Life went on. We wore our Stars of David, but not in shame.

In our town there were about two hundred Jewish youngsters and about one hundred of us were between the ages of ten and eighteen. Excluded from the general community, we formed our own. My schooling moved from the schoolhouse to our living room. Groups of children met and were instructed by young Jewish teachers. Schooling was improvised; the older boys and girls taught the early grades. I was ten years old when I had my first Latin lessons. I still remember "amo, amas, amat" and my introduction to algebra. We read about animals and distant lands. We sang songs in Hebrew which, for me, was a strange language that until that point had been used only in prayer. We dreamed about the faraway land of Palestine where Jews were making a fresh start. Occasionally, a father of a friend would be arrested and would disappear. We had to give away our car. Father was forced to close down his medical office and we had to live off his savings.

Another Jewish family lived in our building. They were simple, poor people who lived next to the butcher's store. Their place was warm and smelled of cooked meat. I don't remember their names, but their daughter Anna and I became friends. I often visited their warm apartment, where we sat around, talked and played cards. In time, we were ordered to give up half of our apartment. We lost two of our four rooms to some insurance office. Our maid, Maria, had to leave us, but she would often come to visit.

Some friends succeeded in leaving the country. They went to Palestine, England, Canada and the United States. It became more and more difficult to get permission to leave. My father was among the optimists and thought that all would soon return to normal. He and his friends liked to joke about Hitler and the Nazis. Unfortunately, the whole thing was far from a joke.

Among the more pleasant memories from this time – 1940 to 1941 – were the summer days spent along the River Vltava. Although we were banned from public swimming, we were allowed to swim along a narrow strip of land by the road. This strip was a half-hour walk from town, or a ten-minute ride by bicycle, and was near a railway bridge. It was called U Vorisku, named after the Voriseks family who owned and leased us the patch between the fields and the river. We bicycled, jogged, walked or ran to U Vorisku. It soon became a hub of activity. Swimming past the shoreline was treacherous, especially for younger children. The older boys had a tiny boat that was used to rescue the daredevils who tried. The water in the river was filthy, with pieces of raw sewage floating on the surface; one never put one's face into the water. Yet it was a place where we could cool off and have fun.

We were permitted to set up benches and changing rooms along the river. We had space for four ping-pong tables and when everything was cleared we even had room for a small soccer field. Someone brought a soccer ball and volleyball net. We played soccer along the narrow field and when the ball ended up in the river – as it often did – it took several minutes to retrieve it. I was ten and would always play soccer with the older boys. I played the defence position. I was small, tough and daring, and stopped every attack on my team's goalie.

My real success, however, was in ping-pong. We had two tables situated underneath a shelter behind the changing cabin. I played as often as I could. There was a tournament toward the end of the summer of 1941. We were divided into three age groups: under ten, ten-to-fourteen, and fifteen and older. I had early success, eliminating most of my opponents quickly. In the semifinals and the finals, I won every game. At an evening ceremony, I was awarded a brand-new white cork racquet and a plaque with my name engraved on it. There was dancing and singing. That evening, I felt that everyone liked me. These youngsters were my friends. There were the Harrys, Jirkas, Pavels, Karels, Rudlas, Lilkas, Ritas, Ankas, Suzans, Lidias and Cecilias. There were Poppers, Kopperls, Kohns, Herzes, Holzers, Frishes, Stadlers and Levys. There were even more, but I have forgotten most of the names. We were young, enthusiastic and mischievous, but we were always good to one another. Great warmth was established among us young people and we developed a deep love and respect for each other.

The two summers of 1940 and 1941 were among my happiest. Some days we worked on the Voriseks' farm, helping with the harvesting. I held a large canvas bag under a chute and filled it with oats or wheat. For our work, we received a large slice of fresh white bread, thickly covered with goose liver and fat.

We all had daytime duties. The older boys and girls were learning trades. Under orders from the Nazis, the Jewish community had to submit information about our properties and compile lists of our addresses, so the younger children, like myself, delivered this information in sealed envelopes. The moment we finished our duties, we would rush to our favourite spot along the river. We played team sports and our friendships intensified. Every moment in the sun was cherished and when it rained we would huddle under trees. In addition to athletics and games, we would sing. Sometimes there were fights, usually ending with someone coming home with a black eye.

When the days began to shorten and the cool air returned, we knew our beautiful summer was coming to an end. Several of the older boys decided that we must not hibernate but continue with our friendships. They started a handmade magazine named *Klepy* (Gossip). It was typed and illustrated and only one copy of each issue was printed. One issue had a picture of me kicking a ball on the front cover. The first issue merely gossiped about our summer activities at the river. However, subsequent issues had stories and jokes. Contributions by the readers were sought and published. All readers were given a chance to read the single printed copy and were asked to comment on the issue. There were twenty issues of *Klepy*.[5] Here is an excerpt from an early issue:

What is the goal and purpose of our Klepy? *First of all, to prove that a healthy spirit and sense of humour is within us and that we are not diminished by the difficulties of our days. We are capable, in moments of rest from our labour, to occupy our minds with worthwhile thoughts and humour.*

During this time, two boys were afflicted with epilepsy. The worst case was Fricek K. He was new to Budějovice, having come from the Sudetenland a few years earlier. Fricek was always with his cousin Erich. They were both ten years old. Fricek had frequent epileptic fits, sometimes as often as every half hour. He would fall to the ground, lie on his back, and emit terrifying shrieks. When this would happen, his cousin Erich would open Fricek's mouth, which was full of froth, and pull out his tongue, caressing his forehead. The sick boy would shake wildly for three to four minutes and then appear to be in a deep sleep for a few minutes. After that, he would get up, looking weak and dizzy. This frightening event occurred many times each day.

Another person who had the same affliction was an older man we called Mr. Papa. He was a confectionery vendor. He had a wagon with candies, apples and chocolate bars. He could always be found in the shade under the large railway bridge. I used to buy a chocolate rum ball from him whenever I could afford it. His epilepsy was quite different. His attacks came only once every two weeks. When they occurred, he would fall on his back, breathing heavily, and lie in this state for almost a full hour. There was nobody qualified to do anything for him, other than give him a glass of water when he finally came to. After an attack, he would not show up to work for a few days. But when he did come back, it was always with a fresh supply of apples, chocolate bars and candy.

The summer of 1940 passed and we had only our memories to keep us warm. We looked forward to next summer – until it came. During the summer of 1941, our lives were in imminent danger. These threats were not from our fellow citizens, but from the mad dictator in Berlin. As the days became shorter and cooler, we cherished each day and prayed that the summer of 1941 would never end. For many, this would be their last summer.

Around this time, we, the Jews of Budějovice, started to take some interest in religion again. Our beautiful, tall synagogue had two steeples and many beautiful entrances and was located in a fine part of the city. It was built in the late 1800s. The Germans could not stand competition from another God, so they blew up the synagogue – completely wiping out any trace of the original building. Without the synagogue, services were held in a large, decorated warehouse. Our rabbi, Rudolf Ferda, inspired the participation of the children, and soon Friday night services were full of girls and boys. A chorus of ten- to twelve-year-old girls and boys was organized and their beautiful voices made many at the services tremble with joy. The boys learned to pray and, both in fun and seriousness, imitated our cantor by holding services at home. Rabbi Ferda was a good man. His long sermons always included the theme that Jewish history winds itself like a red thread through the ages. He spoke in Czech with a German accent, and sometimes we could not keep from bursting into laughter. However, when he ordered us out of the sermons, we were really sorry.

A special relationship developed among the young Jews who were shunned by the general community and vilified in newspapers and on radio. We found new strength and helped each other through the hard times. When a very poor family came to town with many children, room was quickly found to help them. Our family took in a little girl who lived with us for a while.

My father was no longer permitted to practise medicine and spent the summer days working in a friend's garden. He loved it. We worried about what would happen when our savings were gone. We got used to eating less and eating cheaper food: bread without butter, potatoes and, only rarely, meat.

The summer of 1941 came to an end. We still went to U Vorisku in the fall and sometimes in the winter, where we would walk around and look forward to the next summer. But this was not to be. In April 1942, the whole Jewish community (just under a thousand people) were taken from their homes and resettled in the ghetto Terezín (Theresienstadt, in German).

DEPARTURE

České Budějovice was my town, my home. It was there where my Grandfather Alexander sat in his office overlooking the large square and administered justice as a county judge. A stone's throw away from the Black Tower, my father ran his doctor's office where mothers brought their sick children to be helped and where he saved many lives. There were a few grocery and linen shops owned by our Jewish friends that had been passed down through generations. Some friends owned factories, while others worked in them. There was a scrap-iron yard owned by a Jewish family, and there were several Jewish teachers and doctors. These families had lived in the town for many generations – no one considered that we did not belong.

In April 1942, the population of our town fell by nearly a thousand. We had been notified that we were to appear with our luggage at a large warehouse near the railway station. The Jews of Budějovice were a civilized lot – we did not fuss much. We were used to doing what we were told, so we checked into the warehouse, presented our documents, were assigned numbers and prepared for the night. A few children whimpered and some of the older boys started to fool around.

The next day, we were told to board a passenger train that would take us to a gathering place. Our main worry was whether this new place would be in Czechoslovakia. Somehow there seemed less to worry about as long as we stayed in our own country. As the train began to move, we got our first glimpses of the cruel SS men (Schutz-staffel) – the Nazi elite troops who guarded the concentration camps. They were dressed in perfectly ironed uniforms and had animal-like expressions on their faces. One such beast – a high official with many stars on his uniform – inspected the train. Shouting orders in German, he kicked and slapped several people who got in his way.

The train sped north toward Prague, then west. At the end of the day we were unloaded at the gathering place, Terezín. Terezín was an old town that had many soldiers' barracks, massive three-storey brick buildings and several large yards. The town had a moat all around it, making escape impossible.

That first night in Terezín we slept in a large warehouse, body to body, with just enough room to move around on our tiptoes. The next day, all the families were separated. Women were moved to one of the large barracks, and men to another. There was not much time to say goodbye as we had to line up quickly. Food was distributed from large barrels into small pots that were assigned to all the inmates in Terezín. Bread, potatoes and gravy comprised our main daily meal.

We stayed in Terezín from April 1942 until November 1943. The town grew more and more crowded from the incoming transports of Jews from other parts of Czechoslovakia. Old people and sick people started dying quickly. Every morning, bodies covered with white sheets were seen piled up in wagons, waiting to be moved to the crematorium.

At first, we all lived in the barracks, many to a room, sleeping on the floor. Somehow, amidst all this, children were allowed a little fun. We were permitted to play in the yard, to sing and play word games. One of my memories is of a teacher who would sing his and my favourite song, "Spring Will Come Again, May Is Not Far Away."

Terezín was a town of brick and stone, and it had paved streets. There was hardly a tree or flower in sight. One day, a group of us children were permitted to leave the town and play on a small patch of grass. It was early summer. Bees were buzzing and dandelions were in bloom. How wonderful life appeared! Sadness, along with great hope for a future of freedom, brought me to tears. Others felt the same way. Some of the children wrote moving poetry after that day's excursion. A lot of poetry was written by the children of Terezín and some of it survived and was published after the war.[6]

Within several months of our arrival in this strange town, I moved to the address "L417." In Terezín, all the streets going north and south were designated "L" and all those going west and east were designated "Q." So L417 meant house number 17 on the fourth north-south

---

6 See for example Hana Volavkova, ed. *I Never Saw Another Butterfly: Children's Drawings and Poems from Terezín Concentration Camp, 1942–1945* (New York: Schocken Books, 1978).

street. This was not an ordinary house, but a small, two-storey school with wide halls and about ten large rooms. I was assigned to Room 9 on the second floor. In this room there were several double bunks and several single bunks; all were three levels high. These bunks provided sleeping space for forty boys. In the middle of the room, there was a couple of benches and a single long table – there was nothing more. There were only two washrooms in the hall for several hundred boys, so we took turns standing on duty day and night, keeping order, and watching for possible flooding and overflowing.

All the boys in Room 9 were thirteen and fourteen years old. Arno Erlich, a tall, handsome man in his early twenties, was in charge. He was strict, sharp and fair. Just like the rest of us, he was Jewish but not observant. We all loved him and obeyed his commands. Arno had been a Boy Scout leader before coming to Terezín and this was why he was chosen to be our room leader. Some of the other room leaders were teachers or social workers. Most had progressive ideas; some were socialists, some Zionists and some were Czech nationalists who hoped for restoration of a Masaryk-type Czechoslovakian republic after the war.

To keep life meaningful, we were given talks by teachers. This was not really allowed, but no one bothered much to enforce this rule. There were some older professors who would visit us and talk about history, philosophy and math. Some of the boys were really brilliant. I merely hopped along. During one English lesson, I was nicknamed Johnny – a name that stuck with me. From then on, no one called me anything else.

We played games, did our chores and were under strict discipline. We played chess, *Šprtec* (table hockey), Twenty Questions and sometimes we put on plays. We published a newsmagazine once a week. It was written by Stern, the boy with the best handwriting. In the magazine were stories, poems, jokes and drawings. I, too, wrote for the magazine and had several of my poems published.

At certain times, we were allowed to leave the school, either to walk around or to visit our parents. Mother was often sick. Father was the doctor at the L417 school and I saw him often. My brother, Karel, was in another room at the school. On the days we were allowed out of the school to explore the town, we would walk through the back-yards of old houses. We could see people crowded on floors every-where. The big barracks, which were built two hundred years ago, had catacombs (narrow tunnels dug in the ground). Although we were warned against it, we were daring and walked down deep inside the tunnels. On the way back to our house, we would walk past the infir-mary where mental patients were kept. The sight was awful: men and women were lying all over the place, some screaming, others fighting and calling for help. But there was little help around.

One day, with special permission, some of us boys from Room 9 were allowed to join a workforce to tend gardens on the outskirts of Terezín. We were assigned shovels and marched into the country. How wonderful it was to see green fields and hills! We worked until noon and were then allowed to use a shower – a real shower – what a treat! Usually, we just washed in a small basin.

One day, I believe it was November 17, 1943, everybody in Ter-ezín was awakened early. We were told to get ready and ordered to march on the street. We organized ourselves quickly by lining up in a column. Perhaps 40,000 of us were led out the gates to a large valley where we stood in formation to be counted. Toward the afternoon, rumours started to spread that we would all be machine-gunned or that bombs would drop on us. Panic started to spread when darkness fell. No one knew what would happen, but we stood still in long col-umns, five people deep. Finally, late at night, the gates of the ghetto opened. The columns broke apart as everyone began to dash back inside. Many were trampled underfoot and I don't know how many died. All the boys from Room 9 made it back safely and, exhausted, we quickly fell asleep.

The Czech Jews were a talented bunch. There were many famous actors, singers, painters, acrobats and so on in Terezín, and, when possible, they performed. There was a theatre in the attic of an old house and there were evenings of singing that took place in sheds and barns. In the small gymnasium of our school L417, Smetana's popular opera, *The Bartered Bride*, was performed. The conductor sat at the piano and accompanied singers and choruses with happy music. I must have heard it twenty times, either standing or sitting on the floor, as there were no seats.

I even had my bar mitzvah in Terezín. Rabbi Ferda, our rabbi from Budějovice, taught me my Torah portion. He was a bit of an actor, but sincere. He believed that the reason the Jewish people were being punished was because they had left their God. I wondered about that theory. My bar mitzvah took place on June 13, 1943, in the attic of the Dresden Barracks (each barracks was named after a German city). I memorized the whole portion and Rabbi Ferda was very pleased. I got a fountain pen and a small, beautiful pocket watch from my parents, which I treasured until I had to give them up at Auschwitz.

The year and a half I spent in Room 9 was very exciting and, thanks to our leader, Arno, even inspiring. We learned self-reliance. Achievement badges were given for certain tasks. For example, I found it impossible to go without talking for one full day, but I tried anyway. However, the day I tried to remain silent was a day that I went to visit my parents. I was excited about this task and as soon as I saw them I rushed to them and blurted out that I was not to talk that day. Well, that was the end of that experiment!

In Room 9, we formed intense friendships; we discussed everything, and even held ping-pong championships. I was one of the best and represented Room 9 in competition with other rooms. So life went on. We were hungry, and at times sick, but we did not complain. We saw the suffering of the helpless old people around us, who were often left lying on the ground in dirt, waiting for death. Anybody caught attempting to run away from Terezín was executed by hanging in the square. German soldiers were everywhere and they demanded absolute discipline.

We sang songs with lyrics like, "And to resist all the Hamans, we shall break down the gates that keep us in.[7] Soon the day is coming when life will begin again. We shall pack up to go home again, and laugh at the ruins of the ghetto." We staged our battles between the Philistines and the Israelites, with a chorus reciting the story. We re-enacted the David and Goliath fight. We sang Czech patriotic songs and hoped for a happy future.

But it was not to come.

Reports from outside the ghetto talked of the terrible war raging in France and England, and of German forces moving deep into Poland and Russia. We heard that the Germans were losing millions of soldiers in the ice and snow near Moscow. Their victories had started turning into defeats.

More Jews were brought to Terezín from Germany and Holland. Sanitation in the ghetto got worse and food rations were lowered. It was terribly hot in the summer and we froze in the winter. All this was bearable. What was unbearable was the threat of transport from Terezín, eastbound to unknown Poland. When these transports would occur, two to three thousand people at a time were given notice to prepare their belongings and move to an old warehouse. Only two days' warning was given. Fear started to spread about who would be in the next transport. Each transport took two or three boys from our room. After each transport, it was very quiet in our room. Each of us wondered when his number would come up.

On one gloomy day in November 1943, I was handed a little slip. No one knew who made the selections, but there it was – my notice. Soon afterward, my mother came in to help me pack. She was, or at

---

7 In the biblical Book of Esther, Haman is the villain who wishes to murder all the Jews in ancient Persia.

least pretended to be, cheerful. Her favourite Czech song was, "As long as we have our song, we are alive and happy." The next day, my parents, Karel and I checked into a large warehouse with two thousand other people. Only dim lights broke through the complete darkness. I noticed a pretty girl in a yellow sweater in the bunk across from me and she looked at me, too. No one slept much that night. Anticipation and fear filled the air.

So started the journey into the worst part of my life.

Chapter Three

AUSCHWITZ AND BIRKENAU

Auschwitz is a town in southwestern Poland not far from the Czechoslovakian border. To get there by train from Terezín, one passes Prague, continues east toward Moravska Ostrava and then, turning north, enters Poland.

It is an area of coal mines, steel mills, large factories and much poverty. Hundreds of thousands of workers were needed to work in the factories in Auschwitz. What better method to employ unpaid slave labour? When these prisoners became too weak to work, they would be shipped out and replaced by other slaves.

Several miles from Auschwitz, the Nazis built their twentieth-century horror invention: death factories. Unheard of previously in the history of civilization, mass murder contraptions were built by the Germans in the 1940s: gas chambers and crematoria. The location was appropriate – an unknown address with vast flatlands, easily reached by a railway. The name of the place: Birkenau.

Birkenau was our destination.

The train carrying us was a freight cattle train. It had no windows, but there were narrow slits on the side of the train that allowed some air to come in. There was just enough room in our wagon for us to sit or lie down on the floor. We were provided with food for one day and some old blankets. The trip was slow and at times the train stood still for hours. No one knew where we were going or how long it would take. There were old people and children, men and women.

That our family was together provided some comfort. We left Terezín early in the morning while it was still dark. Toward nighttime, some people began to get sick and panic. Arguments could be heard as tension increased. Father had his black doctor's case and during the night he administered injections to several sick people.

It was late at night when we arrived. The doors of the cattle cars were opened from the outside. They had been sealed securely in Terezín before our departure.

Uniformed German SS guards were issuing orders: "Quickly, out of the train. Line up in rows of five along the track!" We noticed men in black-and-white-striped uniforms that looked like pyjamas. These were the prisoners. They told us we were in Auschwitz. Soon we were herded into big trucks. The doors were shut and motors started. The little I could see outside provided a strange sight: long rows of electric lights, a completely flat landscape, high barbed-wire fences in perfectly straight lines and observation posts manned by soldiers who were moving floodlights. It seemed like another planet.

The trucks stopped. In the dark, I noticed that we were all men. The women must have gone in other trucks. We were quickly pushed into a long barracks. Once inside, we were ordered to line up in rows of five again. We were told to put all our belongings in one pile and to undress. That was the last I saw of the beautiful watch and pen I had received from my parents for my bar mitzvah.

We stood naked for a long time, shivering. One of the German guards opened the doors wide, letting in cold air from outside. At this moment, a strange incident occurred. Two men, perhaps in their twenties, were tossed in through the door. They looked yellow and were so thin that their bones could be seen.

They looked almost wild. Someone threw a piece of soap to them and they began to fight over it, thinking it was food. I had never seen human beings behaving like this. They probably had not eaten any food for days.

Then we were moved to the next hall, which had showers. Lukewarm water came from the showerheads for only a minute. I averted my eyes when I saw my father in the nude beside me. After the showers, we were moved again to another long hall. There were piles of torn shirts, underwear, socks, shoes and prisoners' black-and-white uniforms in the hall. We did not have enough time to choose the right sizes, so when we were dressed, we looked completely shapeless. After this, we were brutally shaven all over our bodies and our arms were tattooed. We stood in a line with our left sleeves rolled up. A man came in and with a quick, sharp object, pricked our skin to tattoo our left arms. I received a six-digit number that I still have today, after forty-six years. I became concentration camp number 168329.

It was still dark when we were pushed back into the trucks. We were driven only a short distance beneath the high barbed wire through a well-guarded gate to the camp. This is where we were to spend the next six months.

THE FAMILY CAMP

We spent the next six months in the *Familienlager*, the Family Camp. To my surprise, inside the camp we found Mother and all the other women who had come with us from Terezín, as well as a group of people who had been transported from Terezín three months earlier. By this point, there were probably four thousand people in the camp. It consisted of two rows of about thirty long, wooden barracks. There was a road between the two rows. There was mud everywhere. It was difficult to walk with our loose shoes in the deep mud. Sometimes we would sink into the mud and have to be pulled out.

Of the thirty barracks, one was a latrine and one was an infirmary. Both stank and were full of misery. There were separate barracks for men and women. Children usually stayed with their mothers, but the older boys were put with fathers. In our barracks made of wood, there were three hundred of us, men and boys. Along the entire length of our barracks was a long chimney-like oven, perhaps one metre high and one metre wide. On both sides of the oven there were three-layered bunk beds, each for six people, two people per layer.

Several times a day, for most of the day, we had to stand outside in rows of five, constantly being counted by the SS guards. Their faces were cruel and any movement during the counting was punished with a slap across the face or a kick. I remember a cruel SS officer named Buntrok, known to all as "Bulldog." He kicked and slapped at random and carried a cane with which he used to hit us hard.

Food was dished out once a day. At noon, a large barrel with hot soup was brought out. It was ladled out to each inmate into his one possession – a pot with a handle, known as an *eschus*. With the soup we were given a chunk of bread. In the evening, a barrel of warm, thin tea was brought out and ladled into the same pot. After that, we had free time and could meet with our friends and family. We were given tea again in the morning, but nothing further. On Sundays, the soup was thicker and was served with tasteless, yellow margarine and bread. I saw my mother once a day for fifteen minutes. She had tears in her eyes most of the time.

Living in dirt with only a little water for washing made fleas a problem. All the doctors in the camp, including Father, became responsible for maintaining the hygiene in the camp. They would inspect our clothing in order to kill the fleas and keep the lice under control. One rainy day, all the doctors were called out and accused of not doing a good enough job. They were punished by being forced to run in the rain and do pushups in the mud.

My encounter with fleas was dramatic. I had a warm, bulky sweater assigned to me when winter came. It had such a beautiful design with white, red and grey diamonds. I don't remember how it came to me; it was probably just thrown at my frail body when my turn came for the allotment of winter clothing. The winter of 1943 was severe and my sweater gave me comfort. It had long sleeves and a turtleneck. Some grandmother in Poland or Hungary had probably sat patiently for many hours knitting it for her grandson. This boy most likely did not need it anymore. I wore it all the time. Day and night.

It had broad shoulders and the wool was so soft. It hung loosely over my once chubby but now thin frame. I slept in my sweater. After a few weeks, my whole body started to itch. I scratched a lot. However, other people also scratched. There was little water to wash in and it was always cold. One day, I noticed a large ugly bug on my sleeve. I squashed it, but out came another and another. Horrified, I tore off my sweater. I looked closely. To my horror, I saw hundreds of small animals crawling and carrying eggs. There were hundreds of them – lice – every inch was full of them! Tiny eggs were set deep in the wool. With a vengeance inspired by my rage towards my Nazi tormentors, I pounded at the lice with my fists and I squeezed them with my nails. I stomped all over the sweater with my feet. Kill those creatures! They did not deserve my venom, but then, what had I done to deserve being taken from my home at the age of twelve and thrown into this hell? I could not afford to throw away my sweater so I shook it out, washed it and used my fingernails to kill most of the beasties.[8]

Another problem I developed was swollen and painful gums. My whole mouth hurt and I could hardly open it. This disease was due to lack of vitamins. It made me miserable and I received no treatment. In the spring, my condition improved for a while.

Sometimes during the day, we were free to walk along the road in camp. I met some friends who had previously left Terezín. They were "old timers" and they filled us in on the situation in the camp. We found out that Czech Gypsies were housed in the camp alongside ours and that many of them were children. Ours was the sole camp where families from Terezín were together. Why did we rate that special privilege?

The most curious question we asked of the old timers was about the two large factories, clearly visible from the camp, about two ki-

---

8 Forty-three years later, my memories of those dark nights of 1943 came back when I found and bought a beautiful red, white and grey diamond sweater at a neighbour's garage sale.

lometres away. Each building had a warehouse and a very tall, broad chimney. Heavy smoke often poured out of the chimney. Were these bakeries or brick factories? The answer shook us and made us tremble. "Those are gas chambers," we were told, "where people from the ghettos are killed and burned in the ovens." At first, we refused to believe it. However, several months later, when another transport came from Terezín and was placed inside our Family Camp, it was our turn to tell our friends the true story of the large chimneys. It was a dramatic truth that they, too, could not bring themselves to believe.

Once a month, we were handed a postcard and pencil. We wrote greetings to our families back in Terezín or at home. "...bin gesund zusammen mit den Eltern." (I am well and together with my parents.) Each postcard bore the name of the sender, his date of birth and the location of the camp: Arbeitslager (labour camp) Birkenau bei Neu Berun O.S. We dated these greetings as directed, sometimes six or more weeks ahead. Certainly an ugly omen!

On the other side of our camp was a camp for only men, and beyond that, one for only women. Each camp was separated by an electric barbed-wire fence. Anyone who touched the wire was immediately electrocuted. One day, as I wandered to the electric fence dividing us from the Gypsies, a young boy called me from the other side. "Look!" he said, showing me a large bowl of mustard. "Do you want?" "Sure," I said. "Bring bread," he called back. I always liked mustard and thought it would be good with the dry bread that was all we ever got except for soup and tea. I returned to the same spot at the same time the next day, having saved my full bread ration for the day. I was afraid to put my hand through the electric fence, but the Gypsy boy was not. "Throw the bread." I did and he immediately passed the large bowl with mustard through the fence and ran away. I took the bowl and also ran with it. It occurred to me that I could probably trade some of the mustard for bread. The bowl was heavy, far too heavy. I put my finger into the pot. I did not laugh or cry, but realized I had been taken. There was a thin layer of mustard over the top of a pot full of sand. The Gypsy boy was gone, probably enjoying his extra bread ration. He earned it by sticking his hand through the electric fence.

The winter of 1944 was severe. There was snow and ice. Many people got sick and some died. The days were long that winter; they were cold and dark. Our feet froze in our thin socks and wooden shoes. The women suffered even more than the men. They looked hopeless with their heads shaved, dressed in terrible, loose rags. How can I forget the night surgeons who operated on the frozen feet of one of our friends, a thirteen-year-old boy? His screams must have reached Hell.

One dreadful, endless night, a young man coughed himself to death in the barracks where I lived. He was a sad-looking young man with a pale face and large eyes that gave the impression of a Pierrot (a character from French pantomime). He spoke softly and I could not understand him. Feverish, he shook all over. He coughed, at first lightly, but then continuously and deeper, gasping for air like a drowning man. His wailing spread through the full length of the barracks. It lasted most of the night. Soon, his coughing fits increased. Someone passed him an eating bowl, the type assigned to everyone for his daily soup ration. He spat into the pot, he urinated into it, he vomited into it and when he started to throw up blood the contents turned an ugly red. There was no one to help. In the morning, he was sprawled on the floor, dead.

I must say something about the heroes in our midst. Fredy Hirsch was a dark-haired young man who had organized athletic meets in Terezín and who taught us to have strength of spirit. Fredy was somehow able to squeeze a bit of feeling out of the camp *Kommandant* and arranged for small children to be permitted to spend the cold days indoors. The authorities permitted part of one of the barracks to be opened to children up to age fifteen. Here we could sit on benches in small groups; we could play, read and stay in greater comfort. The older boys and girls, the *madrichim* (youth leaders), organized little groups, played games with us and told us stories. We played word games, exercised a little and sang songs. Someone brought a tennis ball into the camp and we boys divided into teams and played soccer at the very edge of the camp. We children, even then, in the concentration camp, had some spirit left.

At night and during the day, we saw American airplanes flying high in the sky, heading toward the war front. We knew that the Germans had been beaten in Moscow and that they had started to retreat. We learned the latest news from newly arrived prisoners.

By this time, our only thought was, "Will we last long enough to see the next day?" Mother, although not feeling well, cheered us up and at times shared part of her ration with the rest of us. My brother, Karel, got very sick with typhus but miraculously recovered. He was seventeen by then, quite tall and really a good boy.

There was only one successful escape from the Family Camp. This was a miracle and we found out the full story only much later. There was one decent SS guard, a Yugoslav-German named Pystek. He never kicked us or slapped our faces. He even smiled at us (yes, he did, I remember!). The story spread quickly. One day, Pystek and an inmate in the camp rode bicycles wearing SS uniforms out of the camp through the main gate. Their comrades-in-arms saluted "Heil Hitler" as they passed the gate. I know this is true, although whether I actually saw them on bicycles or whether it was just talked about and pictured by all of us in the camp, I don't remember. The two continued down the road, past several checkpoints, into the countryside. They got as far as the nearest railway station, changed into civilian clothes, got on the train and rode away. The lucky escapee, Lederer, made his way to Prague and later joined the underground to fight against the Germans. He survived the war and afterward went to Israel, where he still lives today. What is even more amazing is that Pystek returned to the camp soon after to try his luck once again. This time, he tried to free a beautiful girl he had fallen in love with. Pystek was caught and no one heard a word about him again. After the escape, discipline in the camp was tightened and threats and punishments increased.

While the hard winter weather withered and eased, the mud got deeper. As the spring of 1944 approached, a rumour started to spread through the camp. Transport. This was a fearful word. However, it wasn't a rumour but a reality. In March, an alert was sounded. All those in the camp who had come from Terezín in the transport preceding ours were to move on, though nobody knew to where. Near panic prevailed. By now, there was no longer any doubt. We all knew that the big factories nearby were gas chambers. The chimneys were busier than ever. Heavy smoke poured out constantly, spreading into the surrounding area. The smoke came from the flesh and bones of the burned bodies. Jews. Also some Gypsies, but mostly Jews. One grew used to the smoke and the constant smell, but never to the fear of being the next one burned. This fear was with us day and night. Some days, all appeared quiet, but other days, smoke filled the sky. The busy days were those when new transports arrived. When the factories could not cope with all the bodies, they burned them in large holes in the ground. There were several such holes from which smoke rose, day and night.

March 7 was a date known to all of us. It was Masaryk's birthday and we all worshipped that great man. Perhaps by coincidence, all those who had been in the Family Camp when we arrived in December – the "old timers" – were taken away in trucks and never heard from again. They were gassed, killed and burned. Only a few escaped, some tradesmen who were considered irreplaceable and several pairs of twins on whom Mengele was conducting experiments. The wonderful Fredy Hirsch would not allow others to take his life. He committed suicide just before the end. We wondered when our turn would come. It was a prevailing and tormenting question.

The weather warmed in May. Another transport arrived from Terezín. Like the rest of us before, numbers were tattooed on their left arms with the prefixes A or B. We embraced the newcomers who were as shocked as we had been several months earlier. I recollect walking along the muddy road with one of my roommates from L417 in Terezín, a gentle boy with beautiful handwriting who had printed our weekly newspaper in Room 9. I broke to him the unthinkable, the unbelievable news that those large chimneys spouting smoke day and night were factories of death.

That June, I took off my shirt to get some sun whenever possible. On days when the sun shone brightly, we were all overjoyed, even though our fear was great. Despite our fear and hunger, our children's activities continued. At the edge of the camp there was a large water reservoir and, for a while, we were allowed to use it for swimming.

The reservoir resembled a swimming pool and was at the foot of the *Männerlager* (men's camp), just across from the kitchen. Going into the water was strictly prohibited, but as the saying goes, "boys will be boys." Sometimes, when it was hot and the SS men appeared in a good mood, some brave boy would take a dive into the water. One such day almost ended the life of a boy named Gerhard. Gerhard was a slim, blond boy who had been deported from his beloved Holland to Terezín and then to Birkenau. This quiet boy decided to take a quick swim in the reservoir. As he started his way out of the water on the slippery walls, he was suddenly spotted by an SS man. For either sport or punishment, this SS guard refused to allow Gerhard out of the tank. He stepped on his hands and beat him back with a stick. For the Nazis – who took us out of our homes, took away our parents, put us into concentration camps – the slightest infraction of any rule was punished by the most severe degree. Gerhard started to panic. He pleaded with the SS man. Soon, he began to lose strength. Panting, he started to swallow water. Another boy, Ludek, was nearby and watched in horror. Just then, the SS man disappeared as quickly as he had appeared. Ludek dived in and pulled Gerhard out of the dreadful pool. He stayed with him while he recovered and brought him into our barracks.[9]

---

9 In 1987, Gerhard came from Holland to write down our recollections from Birkenau. When Ludek and Gerhard met in my home, neither of them realized at first that one of them almost drowned and was rescued by the other. When Ludek

The American bombers flew overhead nightly and we heard stories of invasions by English and American armies in France. With increased intensity, transports were arriving and gassing continued. Several months after our arrival, a train station was built at Birkenau-bei Neu Berun. More people were dumped out of the cattle trains. Day and night, the killing went on. Only a few people were given a chance to live; most went out with the smoke. We could clearly see men, women and children advancing toward the large crematoria. No one who entered those buildings ever left. The feared "selection" took place on the railway platform less than a kilometre from our camp. There the drama unfolded as those destined for death were separated from the few permitted to live.

At the beginning of July, there was major panic in the Family Camp. It was now our turn to move on. Would we follow our friends who disappeared in March? No one wanted to admit it, but we all knew the answer. We were handed new postcards to send to Terezín. We were instructed to date them one month ahead. This was ominous. Would we still be alive by then?

Rather than all of us being shipped out at one time, we were shipped out in groups. I remember saying goodbye to Mother. The long barracks was lit with only a small bulb. People were moving about. My brother and I sat with Mother on the lower bunk of the three-tiered bed, so close that our bodies were touching. She knew what her end was to be, but she hid this from her two sons. Instead, she shared a piece of bread with us that she had saved from her supper. But as we three huddled together, we knew where we stood. We did not weep. Mother expressed her lifelong hatred for the Germans and she sang a few Czech songs. "As long as our song lives, we live."

---

started to talk about the event, Gerhard became pale and his breathing became heavy. He began to choke, like he had done in that cool water in the Birkenau pool. He had to leave the room, but when he returned the two men, now almost sixty years old, embraced.

Karel and I joined her. Mother kissed her two boys and sent us to our own barracks.

The first to go were the able-bodied men between the ages of sixteen and fifty. I said goodbye to Father and Karel and watched them march away. It was a hot, dry day. They walked out of the Family Camp at Birkenau in a long column, surrounded by SS guards. Karel was thin and pale, having just recovered from typhus. Father looked a bit better. The column disappeared into the distance. Everyone carried a loaf of bread and whatever small belongings they had. I waved at them through the barbed wire. I heard later that they had been sent to work in a labour camp. I do not know when they died, but I learned later how they died. They had marched for hours on an evacuation march. Karel was not well and he could not keep up with the others. He fell further and further behind. Father stayed with him at the end of the column. Karel fell to the ground completely exhausted. Father tried to help him get up, but the SS guardsman began to shout at them. He kicked Karel, but could not bring him to his feet. The SS guard fired two shots, one at Karel and one at Father. Father died both as a doctor with his patient and as a parent with his son.

The day after I said goodbye to Karel and Father, on July 6, exactly one month after my fourteenth birthday, all boys aged fourteen to sixteen were gathered together. We lined up nude in front of the most feared man around, Dr. Mengele. He was handsome, dressed in the most elegant uniform. As we passed him, he motioned with his finger, either to the left or right. How do I remember the date? "Wie alt bist du?" he asked. How old was I on that day? "Fourteen years and one month," I said in as confident a voice as I could muster. He sent me to the right. I noticed that he sent two smaller boys preceding me to the left. There were almost a hundred boys in the group that I joined. We were told to gather our belongings, quickly say goodbye to the others and form a line at the gate of the camp. We were led into the *Männerlager*, where we stayed until evacuation in January 1945.

Soon afterward, those remaining in the Family Camp were gassed.

They were driven away in closed trucks. Transporting them at night in sealed trucks and circling around the camp may have calmed some, but the end was imminent. At the last moment, people began to fight with bare hands and a few sticks. They were beaten terribly before their deaths. Many were weeping. As we later heard from workers in the gas chambers later, the Czech Jews died singing the Czechoslovakian national anthem, "Kde domov můj" (Where Is My Homeland) and "Hatikvah," the Hebrew song of hope.

My mother died on July 10, 1944.

IN THE MEN'S CAMP

The *Männerlager* was located next to the Family Camp. It looked exactly the same. There were two rows of barracks divided by a road running through the camp. The hundred or so boys who came from the Family Camp to the Men's Camp were housed in Barracks 13. Little did we know that Barracks 13 was usually the punishment cell. We were placed there because there was no space in the other barracks. Unlike other barracks, this block had a fenced-in yard next to it. Gallows stood in one corner of the yard and in another corner was a large sawhorse used for flogging prisoners. It reminded me of the torture doll in Budějovice. Apparently, the Middle Ages were still with us.

The gas chambers were now running day and night. Heavy smoke covered the entire area. Train tracks built from the nearby town of Auschwitz now led right to the death factories. Trains full of people, mainly Jews, arrived every few hours. Thousands were killed daily. The persistent pouring of dark smoke out of the huge chimneys nearby reminded us that life could be snuffed out in a few miserable minutes.

We boys were treated nicely by other prisoners. Both Jews and non-Jews lived in the punishment barracks, mixed together in our miseries. About half of the men were Jews. Particularly, I remember the Russian officers in Barracks 13. They were impressive. Tall and broad-shouldered, these men inspired great respect. They smiled at us and talked to us. In the evening, they hummed and sang their patriotic songs. It made us shiver and even the SS guards were frightened.

The hundred or so boys slept toward the end of the barracks. At 4:30 a.m., we were woken up by a Polish *kapo* named Metek. With a stick, he banged on the bunks singing, "Stavat, stavat, Kurva tvoje mat." (Get up, you whore children.) In fact, he was not a bad guy. The *Blockälteste*, or leader of the barrack, was Bednarek, a German criminal who had been in the camps for seven years by then. He was a man who could be cruel at times and giving at other times.

Soon after our arrival in this camp, the block leaders and *kapos* came to choose runners – *Läuferin*. These boys, the ones whose looks appealed to the "Prominents," or important people in the camp, were assigned to duties as errand boys. They were given fancy outfits and high boots and were allowed to grow their hair. They were moved out to other barracks. Many of the rest of us were assigned to the *Rollwagen Kommando*. Our work was "light." We were human horses, pulling large wooden wagons or pushing them from behind. We would load and unload the wagons with snow in the winter; in the summer, we cleaned the camp or moved coal or whatever else had to be moved. We were up at 4:30 in the morning each day except Sundays, when we could sleep until 5:30. About fifteen boys would work with a single wagon. Our enemies were the heat or the cold, hunger and fear. We worked both inside and outside the camp. At the gate of the camp was a small grandstand for a band. Some of the inmates in the band were renowned musicians, including the conductor Karel Ančerl. The band played in the morning when the inmates marched off to work and in the evening when they returned. I did not see the humour of a marching band inside a concentration camp. When we would leave the camp pulling our wagons, we were made to march to the band.

Our work was tiring and the hours were long. The stronger boys pulled harder than the weaker ones. We did not exploit or steal from each other and we never fought. We were fed only at the end of the day when we returned to our barracks. Before our meal we lined up and waited for *Appell* (roll call). *Appell* was done before the meal and sometimes we stood at attention for hours. If you moved, you were struck by an SS man. After *Appell*, we would line up with our bowls in our hands waiting for our daily meal – a bowl of soup and a chunk of bread. Sometimes we were given a bit of margarine and marmalade with the bread. In the morning, we would line up for a bowl of thin tea. In the evening, after our meal, we sat on our beds or on the long chimney, talking or playing word games. We dreamt about the future. We would discuss politics and religion. Our backgrounds varied. Some of us were from middle-class homes and a few of us from religious Jewish homes. Most of us spoke Czech, some spoke German and a few spoke Dutch. Bedtime came early. As in the Family Camp, there were six of us to a wide three-tiered bunk. In bed, we chattered amongst ourselves and some did what fourteen-year-old boys have always done. At nights in our bunk beds, we would wrap ourselves tightly in our thin blankets so that the large hungry rats that surfaced when it was dark would not attack us.

At noon on Sundays we were given pea soup with chunks of bacon floating in it. Afterward, we were allowed to play with a ball. On one such occasion, I received the one and only injury of my stay in the camp. One of the boys threw a little stone from fairly close by and it landed in the centre of my forehead. All these years later, I still have the scar.

Barracks 11, next to ours, was even stranger than our barracks. This is where the *Sonderkommando* (the special unit) slept, crowded like we were in triple-decker bunks. The men of this special group were strong. They were selected for hard work and strong nerves, and were mostly in their twenties and thirties. They never talked about their work, but everybody knew what they did. They worked in the gas chambers, directing the living to the execution chambers, dragging the dead bodies to crematoria. They knew too much, but they were well-fed. They had access to all the food they wanted: salami, dry meat, loaves of bread, cans of sardines – all the food that newly arrived inmates from Hungary had brought with them on the trains that delivered them to the camp. The *Sonderkommando* were not allowed out of their barracks. However, for a short while, some of us boys defied the order and would sneak inside Barracks 11 at night. The men enjoyed our visits and fed us royally. This was too good to last. Soon an order was made that contact with the men of Barracks 11 was strictly forbidden. Anyone found there would be severely punished. We all knew these terms meant beatings and withholding food. Our visits to the *Sonderkommando* barracks stopped. Our stomachs hurt at night and the smell of delicious salamis felt a thousand kilometres away.

The smallest of us boys was Pauli, who was barely twelve years old. His face was pale and his bones thin. None of us knew anything about his background. Unlike most of us boys who were Czech, Pauli was from Germany. Pauli learned to speak our strange language, though he spoke it with a funny accent. Pauli was the first to disobey the order not to enter Barracks 11 and was caught. He was severely punished. He was dragged to the little courtyard outside Barracks 13 and was thrown to the ground and kicked several times. There was a wooden box in a corner of the yard. They brought this box into the middle of the yard, lifted the lid, and threw Pauli in. Just enough air came in through the cracks so he did not suffocate. He could neither lie nor sit in the box, but had to crouch in an in-between position. His weeping and sighs were loud at first and then grew weaker. He was gasping for air. The boys in the barracks saw it all. This punishment was a warning to others. That night seemed endless; none of us uttered a word. Pauli's whining voice and pleading rang in our ears until we fell asleep. In the morning, no sound came from the box. Pauli, exhausted, had also fallen asleep. But he survived the night.

One day, as I was standing close to the electrically charged fence that divided our camp from the neighbouring one, I noticed a man in the other camp trying to get my attention. Just like all the other prisoners, his head was shaven and he was dressed in the striped camp uniform. He was about forty. I don't remember what language he spoke, probably a mixture of Polish, Hungarian and German. Carefully, I came close to the fence, knowing well that I would be instantly electrocuted if I touched it. The man looked sad and he had tears in his eyes. He asked me my name and age and then told me he had had a son about my age. I did not ask what happened to his son – we both knew and automatically turned toward one of the great chimneys from which heavy black smoke was rolling. My new friend's name was Peter. As we talked, he suddenly raised his hand high and waved in the direction of the camp adjoining ours. A smile appeared on his face. In the distance, I saw a woman's hand returning the greeting. She was Peter's wife. Peter told me that she was bearing life in the camp badly and that he was afraid she would not last much longer. He loved her dearly and wanted to share with her the little food he could save from his own. He threw two pieces of bread over the fence – a smaller one for me and a larger one that he asked me to take to his wife. I picked up both pieces, checking that no one saw me. I ran across the width of the camp to the fence where Peter's wife was standing. She was of medium height and perhaps had been beautiful at one time. With her camp attire and shining head, she was a pitiful sight. I threw the bigger piece of bread to her and she picked it up and ate it. Her eyes were full of tears. I was thinking of my parents – my mother who had been gassed several months ago and my father who had been sent away to do hard labour. At that moment, I did not fully realize the tragedy taking place, day after day. Perhaps my will to survive was stronger than any other feeling. I left Peter's wife as it was time to get back to the barracks. I ate my payment for delivering Peter's message. It tasted good.

From that day on I came back to the fence each day to talk to Peter. He liked me and it was nice for me to have a grownup friend. We would talk for a bit and then I would carry a piece of bread to his wife and get payment for that effort. She usually cheered up when she saw me coming. I always carried the same message to her from Peter, "I love you, and we'll be together again soon."

Like everything in the camp, frequent changes occurred that were usually for the worse. One day, I came to Peter's camp fence, but he was no longer there. The entire camp had been evacuated the previous night. I do not know what happened. Peter's wife also noticed that her husband was gone. She waved at me and I waved back, but I did not go to her side of the fence. I never saw or heard of them again.

Aside from our fear of the gas chambers, hunger and the cold, the most terrible times for us were the punishment days. On these days we were only spectators, but what we saw was horrible. The worst such incident occurred when two men tried to escape. They hid civilian clothes in a small wooden shed near the railway tracks where they worked. They accumulated a flashlight, a couple of knives and food for a few days. However, their escape did not last long. Sirens were heard; their ominous wails filled the air. Motors started; vehicles headed in the direction of the railway. Dogs started their murderous, howling barking and we all trembled.

It was after eight o'clock when three thousand men in the *Männerlager* were forced to stand in rows of five in between the barracks and were not allowed to move. That night, there was no meal. All the men had been standing for almost two hours. The enraged SS men charged at anyone who moved out of line and kicked and slapped at random. Around 8:30, there was a sudden hush in the camp. The marching band at the gate played "Home Sweet Home" and the two men appeared, tied together by their legs. Their faces were black from coal and sweat. They marched slowly, followed by SS men pointing weapons at their backs. The two escapees, George and Manny, carried a cardboard sign with these crudely written words, "HURRAH WIR SIND SCHON WIEDER DA." (Hurrah, here we are again.)

The two men had blood on their faces. First, they were flogged, one at a time. They were held, bent over the sawhorse, their arms and legs tied to it. With his pants down, each condemned man was flogged and had to loudly count each blow as it came down on him. Each blow was administered with a log and each time they were hit, it looked like an electric shock hitting their entire bodies. After fifteen blows their flesh became raw and after twenty-five, blood was flowing. Each man received seventy-five whippings. Two SS men alternated and used all the animal strength they had. One of the two prisoners was a Jew, the other was not. The first man counted to seventy and then just screamed. Then he collapsed and was thrown aside and left bleeding on the ground. The Jewish prisoner knew, just like the rest of us watching, that his punishment would be worse. Four SS men, big and well-fed, took turns hitting him. They hit hard. After 120 blows, the real punishment began. He was thrown on the ground. With long poles, he was beaten over his entire body and head. One of the posts broke, so the angry SS man kicked and stamped and beat with his fists. With his clothes completely torn off, the prisoner was bleeding heavily and his eyes were punctured. Pus came out of his head. His face took on a frightful aspect. This was no longer a man, but a bloody rag. Inhuman sounds emitted from his torn lungs.

We stood there, unable to think.

"Genug!" (Enough!) shouted the commander. "Get a doctor." A doctor arrived. The two men, close to death, were put on a stretcher and taken into the barracks. With crude medicine and dressings, the doctor worked on them the whole night.

No one talked that evening. Two weeks later, both men were hanged on the gallows and the entire camp had to march by and watch the spectacle. Thanks to a request made by the barracks commander – a non-Jewish German prisoner – we boys were not required to march by the gallows.

At this time, the summer of 1944, the Germans were retreating from everywhere. On June 6, my fourteenth birthday, I had learned that American and British troops had landed in Europe to beat back and defeat the Germans. This gave us some hope. The fall's cool weather approached slowly. As the days got shorter and another winter seemed near, there were some new developments. High-flying airplanes above us became a daily event. We heard about the advancing Soviet troops. On some nights, we thought that we could hear distant explosions.

The smoke from the crematoria disappeared. Several weeks later the remaining crematoria ceased to be used and one day, the unbelievable occurred. Work crews began to pick at the two terrible buildings with the large chimneys. The Nazis had started blowing them up, attempting to destroy all the evidence of their deeds. I have a vivid recollection of a brief visit inside one of the gas chambers. Our *Rollwagen Kommando* had to pick some lumber out of the yard of the crematoria, which were partly in ruins. Several of us quickly ran inside the gas chamber. There, we saw a large dark hall made of concrete with thick columns inside the low ceiling. This is the picture I see in my mind today when I enter those concrete garages under large office buildings or apartments.

Cold nights and snow returned. The year 1945 arrived.

The hundred or so boys who had survived the liquidation of the Family Camp were all still alive. Stories of evacuation circulated. Some of the boys were shipped out to other camps, but I think most of us were still together. The guns of the Red Army could now distinctly be heard. We knew the end was in sight, but we also feared that many hurdles were still ahead of us. The gas chambers no longer posed a threat, but our next biggest fear was transports toward the unknown. For most, the unknown proved to be worse than any of us could have imagined. However, we were young and did not feel defeated yet.

In January 1945, just before the Red Army liberated Birkenau, our camp was evacuated and we were shipped out. The final march began.

Chapter Four

THE FINAL MARCH

There are only a hundred days between January 10 and April 22, but in 1945, that period seemed endless. There was no sun – only bitter, cold snow and rain. It was a time when hanging onto life from hour to hour was a major effort. Each of us had hope that the next day our suffering would end. However, each day turned out to be worse than the previous one. In the snow and open coal cars, on endless transports and death marches, one by one we began to fall.

As armies from the east advanced toward the heart of Germany and armies from the west pushed eastward, concentration camp prisoners were dragged from camp to camp, on foot and by train, during the day and at night. We started on foot, several thousand inmates in prison garb. Everyone was given a blanket, a loaf of bread and a can of meat. The first night we marched all night and rested in mud and snow on our blankets during the day. By the second night, many could no longer march. They fell behind and were shot dead. The cruel uniformed SS guards, shouting orders, shot the tired at close range. By the second day of the march, all the food was eaten and the blankets were too heavy to continue carrying. I dropped mine somewhere in the snow.

Finally, those of us who remained – and there were many – came to a small border town with a railway station. It was good to see the train; at least we would not have to march again. The train consisted of an old steam engine and many coal wagons. We were piled into the wagons. There was not enough room for all the men, so they pushed until they were able to close the gate. We could not sit. There were so many bodies standing and leaning against one another. The train stood in the station for hours, perhaps half a day, before it began to move.

It started to snow again. Nobody knew the train's destination or how long it would take to get there. Nobody talked. We stood in silence. If somebody had to urinate, he was shoved along the edge of the wagon where he did what he had to into a pot, poured it from the moving train and was shoved back to his place. There was nothing to eat.

The older men lost their strength and could not stand. Their tired bodies started to lean on others and had to be held up until they collapsed. Then they were taken out at the next station and shot dead by the SS guards. When would it be my turn? How long would I last?

On the second night, I fell, dropping to my knees. I yelled out. The man on whose feet I fell could have kicked me over and I would have been taken out and shot at the next stop. But he extended his arms to me and pulled me up. "He is just a little boy," I heard him say in Yiddish. My friend (a boy whose name I cannot remember) and I held onto each other. When morning came, we were passing through small villages in Moravia. People outside formed a chain. They moved along the train throwing in chunks of bread, rolls and apples. My friend and I shared everything we caught. He was luckier than I; his hands were full, yet he divided it all evenly. We ate what we could and filled our pockets, too. As soon as the SS guards realized what was happening they turned their weapons on the Moravians, clearing the space near the train. The nourishment we caught helped to keep us going for a while.

The next night was bitterly cold. In the open train, we no longer had to stand. So many men had been taken off and shot that there was room to sit and even to lie on the cold floor. My friend was coughing heavily. I fell asleep, covered with some old rags. My pockets had been emptied of every crumb that I had accumulated earlier that day. My buddy was lying near me. He was feverish and babbling. His voice was weak but clear. "Hello, boys," he said. "I have a jug full of hot soup. Come and get it. Hot soup, thick soup. Here is the jug; it's full you see..." He could not go on. His cough was getting worse. "Come and get the good, thick, hot soup." "Shush," somebody shouted at him, but in delirium he walked around holding the imaginary soup jug. Someone kicked him and he fell. It was a slow, long night. When I next awoke it was already light. The body of a little boy, blue from cold, lay next to me. His clothes had been torn off. At the next stop they threw out his body.

While on the train I passed through my town, Budějovice. I could almost see the house where we had once lived. On another occasion, while half-dozing, I heard airplanes above. It was the British. Not knowing what was in the train, they flew along its whole length, machine-gunning it. Bullets were hitting all around me, but I was spared. The train engineer was hit and died in a few minutes. Another raid came, but this time everybody hid under the train. As soon as the planes disappeared, the SS guards forced us back into the train. The few who tried to escape were shot in the back.

During those hundred days, I spent time in two camps in Germany, Oranienburg (Sachsenhausen) and Flossenbürg. When we arrived in Oranienburg, we were herded into a large building that looked like a huge factory. There were several large vats full of water on the floor. Thirsty and hungry, we dipped our hands into the liquid; it tasted salty and foul. Some of us got sick.

The camp was already so crowded that there was no place for us and we were put back onto the train for another long journey. Finally, they found room in Flossenbürg, one of the older German concentration camps. Located on a hill and partly dug into a quarry, it was built into the hillside on several levels with barracks on each level. There were two gallows in the middle of the camp, which were used on frequent occasions. The Flossenbürg camp was inhabited by several types of prisoners, including German criminals, homosexuals, political prisoners and now those of us who had come from Auschwitz. Each type of prisoner was identified by a tag on his lapel. I found that the political prisoners, usually socialists, were decent people. The criminals, all German, were the worst and, together with the SS men, they ran the camp. They were the *Blockältesteren*, the barracks commanders. They acquired certain privileges, such as private rooms in the barracks, supplemental meals and, in some camps, visits to prostitutes. The *Blockältesteren* hung onto these advantages tenaciously by applying the strictest rules in the barracks. Some were crueller than the SS guards.

Fresh snow had fallen the day I arrived in this camp in late February 1945. It was bitterly cold. We were taken for a shower in a small barracks at the edge of camp. It was late at night. After the cold shower, we were chased stark naked through the snow into the barracks that was to be our new home. Prisoner clothes were thrown at us. The barracks was already occupied by other inmates and as newcomers we were not particularly welcome. We were told in no uncertain terms that this camp was a tough place to survive. Discipline inside the camp was strict and unyielding. Punishments for offences were imposed by the SS guards. Minor transgressions were dealt with by their willing helpers, the *Blockältesteren*.

The worst of the *Blockältesteren* was Franz Stocker. We were warned about him when we arrived. "Beware of Franz Stocker, the *Blockälteste*." He was a grey-haired, brutal-looking man of about fifty, but he looked more like seventy. Franz Stocker was angry. He knew that Hitler's whole system was collapsing. It was up to Stocker and others like him to punish their enemies. His great hatred of the Jews was unmatched. He had one expression for us: "Hungarian Jewish swine." We were to be punished. There were about 150 men in his barracks who fit that description; the rest were political prisoners from various conquered countries. According to Stocker, the "Hungarian Jewish swine" had to be segregated from all others. He decided to build a ghetto in the barracks for us. We waited outdoors in the cold March wind as Franz, with the help of prisoners, prepared the ghetto. A corner of the barracks was roped off with sleeping space for perhaps forty.

Franz raged while we filed into our new quarters. We stank, we were ugly, we were swine. He stood on a chair with a rubber hose in his hand. With all his strength he brought down his right hand holding the hose, which landed on our heads. When my turn came, I staggered under the blow, but kept going into the narrow roped-off area. That night, we sat in our barracks huddled like sardines; five of us were packed into each bunk, fifteen people to a three-storey bunk. All we could do was sit up all night, leaning against each other and trying to sleep. At night, many fell down to the ground with a big bang and a painful groan. Some could not get up and were dragged out to the infirmary where several hundred prisoners lay on the ground without the slightest help from anybody. Stocker constantly threw insults at us and would even withhold our already meagre rations. He would hold a rubber hose in his hand and, if any of us upset him, he would let him have it.

Early on our first morning in the camp we were assigned jobs. Mine was to carry goods from one part of the camp to another – clothes, building materials, etc. I was weak after all the travel of recent weeks. A large bundle of blankets was thrown at me to take up the hill. I became faint and collapsed. Someone behind me picked up the bundle, leaving me on the ground. I recovered and went back to carry more blankets.

While I was in Flossenbürg, one of my fellow prisoners was a palm reader. I allowed him to tell me about my future. It was good. He said I would survive. That news lifted my spirits considerably.

One cold night, I saved half my bread ration for the next day. I carefully put it into my *eschus*, covered it with a small rag and slept on it. I should have known better! In the morning the bread was gone.

I do not remember how long we stayed in this camp. The scheduled time to evacuate Flossenbürg coincided with the approach of the American army tanks and artillery. As the American army closed in on Germany, Flossenbürg was suddenly evacuated. Everyone had to leave. We set off on yet another march in the long columns. The most pitiful were the sick. They, too, were chased out of the barracks. Many could hardly walk and were machine-gunned in the nearby fields and quickly buried in the ground. We were wet from constant rain. Few survived. One of the survivors was Franz Stocker, though not for long. His cruelty and loathing was not forgotten. He met his end – he was hanged from a tree, condemned by those he had tortured.

On the hundredth day, it was pouring rain, but the spring air fought its way through the fog. Trains were no longer running as all engines had been destroyed by attacks from Allied planes. The sound of guns was always present. On foot, we trudged through fields with the SS guards still pointing their guns behind us. We spent the last night of the march in a barn, sleeping a few hours on some straw. At this time, there were probably no more than two hundred of us in that group and most were strangers to me. At dawn, we were awakened to prepare for another day of a death march. Somehow, I just kept going, thinking of nothing more than the day when it would all be over. I kept going, step by step, hour by hour. At about noon, I noticed that our SS guards had become quite disturbed. These big cowards who, only a few hours ago had been shooting exhausted prisoners, suddenly started running. As we left the small forest and came into the open, a strange sight appeared ahead.

A long column of roaring tanks began to approach us. Fearing, at first, that they were Germans who were withdrawing, we started running away from them. The tank commanders waved and we stopped running and turned toward them. A large silver star on each tank signalled to us that these men were Americans. I wept briefly, but there was no time for this. A young man, an American soldier, arrived in a jeep. He spoke Yiddish. Waving his gun, he gathered the group of us and took us to a small nearby farmhouse. He ordered the farmer to feed us and to put us up. That night, April 22, 1945, the war, for me, came to an end.

Some questions remain: How did I survive when so many died? The easiest way to answer would be to say that God was with me, though I cannot accept this explanation because it raises more questions than it answers. Why, if God was present in Europe in the 1940s, did He allow the rise of the Nazis, the destruction of cities, the death camps, the murder of millions of Jews and others? More than forty million people died in camps, battlefields and bombed cities. Where was God? Our Budějovice rabbi, Rabbi Rudolf Ferda, believed that we Jews were punished for leaving our religion and the moral teachings of the Torah. Perhaps there is some truth in this, but would a just God punish so severely and unmercifully?

In practical terms, I would say that 95 per cent of my survival was due to luck, luck at being in the right place at the right time. The remaining 5 per cent was due to my physical stamina, my will to live, and to some of the moral qualities taught to me by my leaders such as Arno Erlich, my leader in Terezín. Not least was the foundation of my happy childhood before the war and the inspiration of my parents.

Even though I cannot believe that God selected me to live, I am grateful that I survived.

Chapter Five

I was not yet fifteen when, somewhere in the wet forest of blood-soaked Germany, my ordeal came to an end. I was alive! I spent a few days resting and regaining strength in the old farmhouse where I was placed by the Yiddish-speaking GI. Under his orders, the German family had to look after me and a few other former inmates. That first night, I slept in a bed while tank battles raged all night. My first meal went through me like a sieve. Then the time came to start my return home. I still had some small hope that someone from my family was also recuperating and heading home.

My journey started on the front bumper of a jeep driven madly by a black American soldier. I held on for dear life. We soon came to a village where a group of about forty men were placed into a large military truck to be driven to the Czechoslovakian border. How could the driver have known that he should have gone east? We ended up driving west. After about two hours, we arrived at the city of Nuremberg. This was where the Nazis had held their great parades. Here the virtues of hatred and war had been glorified. Now it was a sight to behold. Long blocks of destroyed buildings, some still smoking from fire, covered the entire city. This was the end of the war that Germany had forced upon the world.

Two days later, we arrived at the border. We saw the red, white and blue flags and the smiling faces of people in the streets. The beginning of May had always been cheerful here, but in 1945 it was different: a new era was born.

Only a few of our group were headed for my hometown of Budějovice. There was no transportation. Trains were not running and buses had no fuel. Three of us were given a ride in the back of a panel truck. As our vehicle, puffing like an old woman, came to the crest of a hill, the gears failed and so did the brakes. I saw the driver jump out. The rest of us were stuck in the van and began our journey down the hill. I thought it was almost funny that my life would come to an end this way. Fortunately, this was not to be. We landed in a shallow ditch, with the van on its side. The three of us started to walk and we walked for hours. Finally, we arrived at a tiny railway station and begged for a ride to Budějovice. After a while, an old steam engine appeared with an engineer and coal stoker and they offered us a ride in the tiny locomotive. As a child I had always admired steam trains, and now I was in one, going home. There was nowhere to sit, so we stood all the way. A fellow traveller, an older man named Polevka, never stopped talking. He is the only person I have ever met who said it was better in the camp because he did not have to fight with his wife.

When we finally arrived in Budějovice, my face was black from coal and my clothes were torn. It was early evening and I walked through the town, unnoticed, to my old address, Jírovcova 11.

I knocked on the door of the Kocers', the couple who had owned the building I had lived in. A young woman opened the door. Yes, she recognized me. She was the wife of one of the Kocers' sons. She asked me in and said I could stay and look for my family the next day. First, I had to have a bath. A real bath, in a tub. My first one in three years! Then Vera fed me and she and Vojtech, her husband, made a bed for me in their own bedroom, on a couch in the corner.

Our beautiful apartment was empty. Shortly after liberation, a young man and woman I had met asked me why I never smiled. "How can I?" I replied. Now that hunger and the fear of death receded, the pain and sadness of living through hell and losing all those I loved was great. I waited for someone from my family to return. No one did. I was not really surprised. Only a handful of our people returned. One of those who did return was my mother's cousin, Karel Ofner. His wife, Pavla, was not Jewish, so he had been treated a bit better than others. The Ofners lived in a gloomy, dusty apartment with a washroom at the end of an unlit hall. These kind people took me in. There was not much to eat. Pavla made a thick soup every day and served it with bread and potatoes.

I wandered alone through the streets of Budějovice. The smell of the town was the same. The old Black Tower, built centuries ago at the edge of a large square, was even blacker from the soot of war. A few people stopped me in the street and said, "I remember your father. He saved the life of our child." The signs on cinemas, at the entrances of parks and the municipal pools, saying "Jews Not Allowed" had been removed, but there were no Jews left in town. Uncle Karel thought of my future and so did I. I bought a beginner's Latin textbook, and Uncle and I visited the high school to enrol me for the next season. The halls of the school were dark and the principal, who always wore an oversized hat, was unpleasant. He said that he could not enrol me because the law banning Jewish students from schools had not been cancelled. Did he not know that the war was over and that the Nazis had lost? Stunned, we said nothing and walked out.

The summer came and with it returned walks with my childhood friend Zdeněk . We went to the swimming pool and helped out in the fruit shop across from my old home. I walked alone to the U Vorisku area along the Vlatva River. Four years ago, this place was full of happy noise and life. Now, there was not even a sound. My emotions wavered between utter defeat and the feeling of victory over Hitler.

There was not much to eat, but in comparison with the war years, it was paradise. There was no longer any danger to my personal safety. I was happy to be alive.

In August, I went to a small village named Dubné for a month of recovery. It was a month full of sunshine. The family who owned the local grocery store took me along as a companion for their eleven-year-old son, Jena. He had three older sisters who were busy with their own lives. We went swimming in a water hole nearby and took bicycle rides to the nearby town of Hluboká. I had my first "date" then, which was a complete disaster. Jena arranged it with the prettiest fifteen-year-old village girl. We met in the dark in the village square. We stood there next to each other, she looking one way and I looking another. I was too terrified to utter a sound and she did not help. After a few minutes, which felt like forever, we walked away. The next day, Jena and his eleven-year-old friends wanted to know whether we had kissed. I learned that the village kids knew more of that type of life than most, but I was far from ready for a girl.

At the end of the summer, I thanked my hosts and returned to Budějovice. Karel Ofner had good news for me. My aunt Anna Weiss, my father's sister, had returned from Terezín where she, her husband and daughter, Marianne, had been allowed to remain until the end of the war. Their survival was miraculous. Their son, Willie, had hid in his girlfriend Sylva's apartment in Prague during the war. His younger brother, Hans, was the kinder of the two brothers. During the war we were both in Terezín where he worked as a cook. When he could, he would slip me some extra food. Hans was later sent to Auschwitz where he died.

Aunt Anna and Uncle Max were now living in Prague and were willing to give me a home. Uncle Max's health was not good and he died shortly after I arrived in Prague. I moved to the fine district of Vinohrady, into a large apartment building with my strict aunt and two girls in their early twenties, both camp survivors. The time to rebuild my life had begun.

The rest of my family was gone. My uncle Franz, his wife, Irma, and their two children, Freddie and Fanci, Uncle Leopold Jung and his entire family, my aunt Randa and grandmother Hermine – they all ended up in the gas chambers.

LIFE IN PRAGUE

Before the war, visiting Prague from Budějovice with my parents was one of my greatest enjoyments. To live in this big, beautiful city would have been a treat under normal conditions. For me, however, it was not all joyous. I admired the wide boulevards with imposing old buildings, the many parks and theatres, the sights of the meandering Vltava towered over by the castle Hradčany, the graceful bridges and the concert halls, where I spent many hours of pleasure. I felt sadness over losing my family and having lived through such inhumanity for reasons that I will never understand.

I was fifteen years old and schooling became my most important concern. I was enrolled in a *Gymnasium* (high school) not far from my new home. Having not been to school since leaving Budějovice in 1942, I found it very difficult. In particular, I feared Latin, physics and math. I was placed in the first grade of the school (equivalent to Grade 9 in Canadian schools). Our teachers, called professors, were paranoid primadonnas whose daily joy was to humiliate their students for whom they felt real hatred. To be called to the blackboard unprepared was like a punishment. Marks were based on such occurrences and there was no opportunity for second chances. Of course, our professors had their favourites, but I was not among them. Nevertheless, I worked to the best of my capabilities and eventually my marks began to improve. Classes took place from eight a.m. until two p.m., and on Saturdays we got off at noon. From 1945 to 1948, I struggled through school, trying to catch up on what I had missed during the war.

Making friends was also difficult for me. My aunt was strict and did not want me to look for the friends I had made in the camps. It was her belief that the only way I could live a normal life would be to forget all that had happened in the past and become a "Czech boy." Well, my attachment to Czech history, literature and particularly music was very strong and I had never really spoken another language. But it was not in me to drop my Jewish past, although my religious commitments were few.

Every Saturday, dinner was served just after the noon news, which we all listened to with great anxiety. Aunt Anna served meat and potatoes. The guests were always her son, Willie, and his wife, Sylva. I liked those meals. Conversation was on a high level. Willie was a bright lawyer and worked for an oil import business. Sylva was an actress and knew the great playwright Karel Čapek personally. Her father had been a member of the pre-war parliament. Willie and Sylva would dazzle me with their erudite talk about business and, more important to me, theatre and music. They were busy with social contacts and always had some interesting gossip. Sylva gave me English lessons once a week in their elegant apartment near the Vltava.

Every Sunday, a similar type of meal was served to my aunt's daughter, Marianne, and her husband, Charles. When they were over, we talked more of our immediate concerns, such as how to live in the post-war society. Charles was completely practical and totally unsentimental. He was quick to tell me when I did something wrong. I would get annoyed when too much conversation centred on that subject. I was the opposite of Charles. I was impractical and sentimental. I liked to daydream and did not like to be told what to do. After all, I was sixteen. I knew that I didn't have many friends. Football and hockey were not as important to me as they were to other boys my age. When I read, I liked to read books that were meaningful to me. Charles taught me Latin once a week in his apartment. Charles and Marianne devoted great effort to me and I knew they cared for me, but still I preferred our Saturday company.

In Prague, I experienced exciting city life with its many cultural activities. I was introduced to music by my aunt and her family when we attended a gala concert devoted to Beethoven. From that moment on, I longed for more. My sadness, rage and depression were exposed by the compositions and followed by the uplifting joy of the music. I discovered opera. As a combination of drama and music, I considered it to be the highest level of art. On Saturday afternoons, I would frequently stand for two or three hours in the gallery of the ornate National Theatre, charmed and excited by what went on in the orchestra and on stage. I would then walk, elated, through the busy streets of the wonderful city. During one of our classes at school, we were all required to prepare a short talk on a subject of our choice. I chose Beethoven, who had struggled in his life and overcame his rage. After my talk, one of the brighter boys said that I was far too young to waste my interest on such subjects and that I should leave this to "older women."

In 1946, I spent July at a Boy Scout camp, sharing a tent with a classmate and friend, Pavel Gottlieb. His father had died in Auschwitz, but Pavel had spent the war with his mother in Prague. Our camp was located at the edge of a forest along a meandering river. That summer, political unrest in the world started again. The war had ended only a year earlier and many people had suffered and lost their lives. Talk returned to destruction. Stalin was raging. He was a great hero to so many, though a mistrusted dictator to others. In his own land, the Soviet Union, Stalin held tight control over the people and the army, and his quest to expand his power began. Farther away, the United States had dropped two atomic bombs on Japan and were continuing more tests in the region. At camp, we all talked about this, wondering if it would, as many believed, commence a chain breakup of all molecules in the entire world and end it all?

My best friend, Fricek Adler, his sister Hana and their parents returned to Czechoslovakia. They had survived the war, first by going to Norway and then to Sweden, always moving ahead of the German armies. While my father had been an optimist, expecting the bad times to blow over in a few months, his friend Hugo was a realist. It was Zdenka, Fricek's mother, who had pushed their family from country to country. After the war, the Adlers lived in a tuberculosis sanatorium in the mountains where Fricek's father was the director.

In August, I took a long trip to visit the Adlers. From the moment I arrived, my admiration for my friend Fricek returned. Those were happy days. We went swimming and bicycle riding. We read books and talked and laughed a lot. The Adlers lived the life of "gentlemen farmers." They grew vegetables and raised ducks and rabbits. Hana was thirteen and had blossomed into a very pretty girl. We talked about politics and current movies and listened to records. The new State of Israel, the first Jewish state in two thousand years, was struggling to get established. Hugo looked toward it as the future for the Jews, just as my father had. Though my father had not acted, Hugo did. First the Adlers escaped Hitler and they were ready to escape again, if necessary. They left to settle in Israel shortly after its founding.[10]

In 1946, hope for a free and democratic society in Czechoslovakia was not yet lost. A free election held in the spring brought in a coalition of Communists and other parties. However, Fricek and I were having too much fun to burden ourselves with this. I returned to Prague with increased self-confidence.

DARKENING CLOUDS

The year 1947 came quickly. The streets of Prague were covered in snow and for the many old-fashioned streetcars, moving around the

---

10 My friend Fricek, now named Yaakov, followed in his father's steps. He became a medical doctor and eventually rose in the army ranks to become the Assistant Surgeon-General of the Israeli army. But this was many years later. He was the Chief Medical Officer of the Israeli army in the Sinai Desert in the 1973 Arab-Israeli War.

city became difficult. The rooftops of the Malá Strana and Hradčany displayed unusual beauty. There was hope in the air.

I started a notebook, and on the first page I wrote about my hope for peace and understanding among the wartime allies. My life at school improved and I made a few friends. I read Paul de Kruif's *Microbe Hunters*, *The Story of San Michele* by Axel Munthe, the biography of Madame Curie, *The Three Musketeers*, all of Čapek's books and a romantic book about the life of the greatest of the Pierrots. I also saw a movie once a week. I favoured the serious movies, but also light Hollywood musicals. Once, as I stood in a line for a movie, I overheard a conversation that shocked me deeply. The people standing in front of me talked about the horrible Jews who came back after the war and wanted their possessions back. I saw memorable films, like *Alexander Nevsky*, *President Lincoln*, *Les enfants du paradis* and *Stairway to Heaven*. My interest in music did not diminish and I became familiar with composers other than Tchaikovsky and Beethoven. I came to like Prokofiev, Debussy and Bartók. Life in the 1940s was harsh; dissonance and disharmony expressed the mood. My happiest days were when I went walking through the city or bicycling with friends. Then I felt like everyone else.

Unfortunately, post-war joy did not last long. Czech Communists, backed by the Soviets, became aggressive. They wanted all the power – sharing was not on their agenda. Stalin's rule became increasingly cruel. Stalin wanted as much land around the Soviet Union as possible. Big power conflicts between the East and West, between Russia and the United States, started to affect our lives. The threat of another war loomed. There were long discussions of whether Communism was better than democracy, and vice versa. The Iron Curtain started to descend between East and West. The system in the Soviet Union was to become the norm in all Eastern European countries – if not installed by election, then by power of the sword. The radio, newspapers and billboards aimed propaganda at us daily. Who was to preserve freedom and achieve prosperity for all, the Communists or their opponents? Who were the opponents? Were they the fascists and greedy capitalists that the Communists said they were? People were divided, each suspecting the other of furthering opportunistic goals through political feelings. I was confused. Was it not the West that betrayed our homeland and that was now arming itself with atomic weapons? When do things become so bad that freedom should be given away for expediency, and when are false arrests justified to protect the good of a nation? There were pure, decent idealists who threw themselves 100 per cent behind Communism. They attended lectures on Marx and went to demonstrations against the opponents.

Another summer passed. My aunt Anda came to visit from Innsbruck. She looked sad and tired. Her sister and brother had both been murdered by the Nazis. She knew, like everyone else, that life would never return to what it used to be. Her husband, Robert, who was not Jewish, had helped hide her during the war. In the Austrian army, Uncle Robert rose to the rank of colonel, only one step below a general, but when the Germans occupied Austria in 1938, he was immediately retired because of his Jewish wife. From then on, he devoted his life to studying history and chemistry and to protecting his wife and their daughters, Eva and Pully, from the Nazis. Though they encountered many tribulations, they all survived the war. During Aunt Anda's visit, we went to the National Theatre to see the joy of Czech music, *The Bartered Bride*. I stood in line for hours to get tickets – Jarmila Novotná, the greatest living Czech soprano, had come from New York to perform.

I spent August with the Adlers in the hills of Moravia. Fricek and I went for a long bicycle trip through Moravia. There was so much beauty in my native land! We made it to Brno and Olomouc and Hodonín, the birthplace of the humanist president and founder of modern Czechoslovakia, Tomáš G. Masaryk. We all wished we could hear his wisdom now – we needed it so badly. When we returned, I almost fell in love with Hana, who, at fourteen, was beautiful. I went for long walks with her. There was something telling me that life would take another turn. I lingered in the lovely woods and streams.

In the fall I entered the sixth year, known as *sexta*, at the *Gymnasium*. This was serious schooling, only two years away from the feared *Maturita*, or matriculation. Then I would have to decide what to do with my life. Studying medicine and following in the steps of my father would be the ideal, but would I be capable? Would my lack of financial support stand in the way? Would the threat of political upheaval hinder me? Would I be willing to sell my integrity for a membership in a political party? Would my Jewish and bourgeois background impede my progress? Did I express the wrong political views? I read newspapers daily, cutting out important statements by politicians. Economically, things were not going well. Food supplies were diminishing; there were long lines at stores. School was closed on cold days due to the coal shortage. My aunt and I began to worry that someone politically well-connected might try to grab our beautiful apartment. Who would stand up for us?

The United States offered Czechoslovakia economic help under the Marshall Plan. Under pressure from Stalin, we did not accept the aid. The Iron Curtain was drawn lower. I attended a concert of modern orchestral music. The cacophony of Honegger's symphony was exactly what we were living.

Then my lucky break came. I was offered the opportunity to leave the country and settle in Canada, assisted by the American Jewish Joint Distribution Committee and the Canadian Jewish Congress (working with the Jewish Immigrant Aid Services and other agencies). I was ready. I was told that as a Jewish orphan living in Europe, I qualified for entry into Canada – a country I knew nothing about, a place where I knew no one. All I knew about this country with the strange name was that it was in North America.

I applied.

Around Christmas 1947, I went to Budějovice for a few days. Then came the so-called February 1948 Revolution, setting Czechoslovakia back into the Middle Ages for many years to come. On March 12, 1948, a group of thirty war orphans under the age of eighteen left Prague by train. I was among them. That day also saw the funeral of Jan Masaryk, the gentle son of the great and beloved Tomáš G. Masaryk. Jan, who was foreign minister, either killed himself or was killed by Russian agents because he wanted to keep his country free. As I waved goodbye to Prague, to Europe, to the old world, I began to look forward to a new life in Canada. I was almost eighteen and I had much to live for.

Chapter Six

EMIGRANT – IMMIGRANT

So many people in the twentieth century made the move from their homeland to a new land. All longed for a visa for North America. Mine arrived in 1948. Had it been issued a few years earlier, my entire family could have become Canadian and would have survived the war.

I never considered myself homeless, a refugee or a displaced person. The choice to leave my native land was my own. I never regretted it. Those who make the same trip now, in these days of instant travel, leave their homes at noon and arrive before supper. We left Prague in early morning by express train and, after travelling for about sixteen hours, arrived at the harbour of Bremerhaven in northern Germany. The trip across the choppy North Sea was rough. The small ship was tossed hither and yon. There were about thirty of us in the group, mostly boys. We were all survivors, orphans.

Once we landed in England, we boarded a train to London. As the train approached, I was able to see the big city of London, the dream of all my classmates in Prague. For two days we stayed in a dilapidated warehouse in Cheapside, in the miserable East End, full of poor people living in slums. A few of us ventured out to see the town

– Buckingham Palace, the Tower of London, the famous avenue Piccadilly and Leicester Square. While in Trafalgar Square, where Admiral Nelson sits high on a pillar protected by roaring lions, we noticed a little man crossing the road to talk to us.

"You refugees?" he asked. "Yes," we replied. "Jewish?"

"Yes," we said.

"Come home with me and meet my family."

We went by the underground to visit Phineas Goldenfeld, his sad, greying wife and their two children, Regina, a girl of eighteen with thick glasses and dark hair, and Lennie, a boy of eleven.

"These boys survived the Nazis and lost their parents," explained the little man to his family.

Excited, Lennie ran into the next room and returned with a toy gun. "I will shoot them all." He was hard to contain. Mrs. Goldenfeld served a modest meal and Phineas took us back to Trafalgar Square. My contact with that family continued and on each subsequent visit to London, we met again.

Canada was willing to take us in and the Canadian Jewish Congress paid our passage. After two days in London, we were off to Southampton by train. In Southampton, a large ship from the famous Cunard Line, *Aquitania*, awaited passengers. She had been a troop carrier in the war and had accommodated over eight thousand troops on her overseas journeys. Once inside, I felt like a movie star. The ship was like an enormous hotel with hundreds of bedrooms, dining rooms, theatres and ballrooms. It was full of people of all descriptions. My first meal in the ornate dining room, which consisted of many courses, was also my last one. Once we started to move, my stomach began to feel like a whirlpool; it started to churn and I soon found myself on the upper deck, throwing up. Then I went into the dormitory room, where a bed was assigned to me, and I stayed there for the next two days. The trip lasted five days, in the worst of winter weather. Waves as large as an apartment building were tossing the poor *Aquitania* from side to side. The creaking of the walls had me almost convinced that I would never see Canada but would drown in the freezing water of the Atlantic Ocean. However, on the fifth day, my fellow passengers urged me to go out on the deck. I saw land again, a little speck that grew larger and larger until we docked. This huge country was Canada – my new home.

Into Another World

Into another world waves brought me;
Goodbye Europe with old churches
Away from the crooked streets
And mattresses full of sweat…
Into a new world a ship brought me
Wave farewell to those left behind
They would also like to start again
But must stay behind to guard against…
Into a new world I was brought by a dream
Never to see blood spilled again
But can I really throw away
The dreams that soiled my youth?
Will I ever return to the old?
Will I ever see the stones of my fathers?
Will I have to return
To fight the old wars once again?

TORONTO

After disembarking, we travelled by train through endless flat fields covered by deep snow. After a stopover in Montreal, we arrived in Toronto. There were perhaps twenty of us. A man on the train recognized us as refugees and gave us each two dollars so we would not arrive at our destinations penniless. Our trip ended at the beautiful, cavernous Union Station. Some of our group had stayed in Montreal, others remained in Toronto and others headed to Winnipeg.

Toronto of the late 1940s was a medium-sized city with straight streets. It was full of small, private homes located outside the downtown area. There were practically no apartment buildings like there were in Europe. The houses near the downtown area were close to one another and dilapidated. Further out were larger villas surrounded by gardens. This was a country inhabited by English descendants, so each home was a castle with flowers.

At the foot of the city lay the large Lake Ontario. In contrast with the cities of Europe, however, the lake was not part of the city. In the downtown area there were unattractive, medium-sized office buildings and stores. Unlike in European cities, people in Toronto lived relatively far from where they worked or shopped; there was hardly any housing downtown and only a few large hotels. There were few neon signs and only a few movie houses and restaurants. To my sorrow, there were only a few theatres, concert halls and art galleries in town, and none were in the glorious European design. A few people had private automobiles. To get around, one had to take streetcars, which were, to my eyes, far more modern and efficient than those in Prague. Lighting in the evening was poor. After all, only a hundred years earlier, there were only a few muddy streets here and a very small population.

Our little group was housed in a large home referred to as the Reception Centre. The centre was serviced by volunteer Jewish women. Later, this became a Jewish library. Those first few days in Toronto, we did not venture far. I realized that learning English was a priority. A few teenage girls came by in the evening to talk to us. I became friendly with a seventeen-year-old girl, much taller than I, who was from a very poor family and whose concerns for humanity led her toward socialistic ideals. We took long walks and I tried to convince her that socialist ideology, which on the surface supports "the people," was merely something that the Communist Party used for its own unfair and inhuman practices. My English was too poor to express all that.[11] It was April and school was still in full swing. I was urged to enrol in a nearby public school and actually sat for a few days in a class of twelve-year-old boys, just listening. I found this experience not only boring but also humiliating. After all, only a few months earlier I had been translating Latin passages of the poet Ovid.

A few words about some of my travel companions with whom I still maintain contact. Tomy N. was two months older than I. He was handsome, with a fine, chiselled nose and chin. Tomy was popular and successful with girls. Later, he was successful with money. He never suffered from self-doubt and depression, as I did. At times I envied him. Then there was Alex S. Nothing ever bothered him. When I first met him in Prague, he lived with a sixteen-year-old girl who expected him to marry her, a subject not even remotely considered by Alex at that time. Alex was a strong, good-looking boy with a hearty laugh. In Toronto, he became a barber and for years I travelled across the city for a haircut and to be cheered up by him. There were also a few girls in our group. One of them, Miriam, remained my long-time friend. She was a wonderful person who, at the age of fourteen, had been badly injured in Auschwitz and yet survived. Miriam had a limp when we first met in Prague. She was the spirit among us. Always cheerful, she sang when times appeared bad. She was from an observant Jewish family in Trieste and she spoke Slavic languages as well as Italian. In Toronto, Miriam was taken in by an Orthodox family and married fairly young. By 1991, she was a grandmother of ten children.

The brilliant sunshine during my first spring in Toronto warmed me up and prepared me for a better future. My first job was as a busboy in a doughnut shop. I earned enough for room and board and saved for a brand-new bicycle. I turned eighteen on June 6, 1948. I did not know that much of what was ahead of me would be good.

---

11 Many years later, this girl married a man she met at one of the socialist gatherings. He eventually became an alcoholic and left her alone with six children.

While the battles of ideology intensified in my old homeland, I focused on my new life in Canada. As a new Canadian, I learned the ways of independence. I had to get a job to pay for my education and to settle into as normal a life as could be hoped for. I did not become a medical doctor as I had dreamt of as a boy. Instead, I obtained a certificate in the respected profession of accounting. As a chartered accountant, I worked steadily, earning a satisfactory living until my retirement in 1989, more than forty years after my arrival in Canada.

I never gave up my love of music and the arts. While young, I read the major European authors, but I never really became an educated man. My doubts about myself and humanity remained with me. I was always aware of the struggles of other people, and this caused me sorrow. The peaceful life that I have enjoyed personally never became a reality for the world.

The greatest day of my life was June 21, 1958. It was on this day that I met my life partner, Nora, whom I married one year later in a synagogue in a small Ontario town. She had come to Canada with her parents from Czechoslovakia just before the outbreak of the war. Now, decades later, I can look back on our lives with satisfaction. We brought three wonderful daughters into this world and are now the grandparents of ten.

For twenty-five years, we raised our family and created a good home for our children. While I worked in a government job, Nora brought up our children. She never used her university degree as a hotel manager but applied her knowledge in practical ways in looking after our family. Her active mind has been engaged in a variety of endeavours for the community. Since my retirement in 1989, I also participate in many volunteer activities. We have enjoyed our country home for many years. We love gardening and reading. Nora does handicrafts and we just enjoy being together.

I returned to Europe many times in search of beauty and enjoyment. Once, in 1956, I travelled alone on a "grand tour" of the major European capitals. On later trips, I was always accompanied by my beloved wife, Nora. Sometimes our children accompanied us. In 1989, we were permitted to visit the Czech Republic, the land of our births. Italy and Israel remain our favourite countries to visit. We love Italy because of its beautiful landscape, artistic achievements and way of life. For Israel, our feelings are emotional: here is a land where our people have survived and thrived under such difficult circumstances. Our daughters have followed us in our love of travel and they, too, have special feelings for Israel.

God has been good to me. I do not deny His existence, but pray to Him only with great doubt.

Epilogue

May 5, 1990, was a day to remember. At Kibbutz Givat Haim in Israel, about four hundred visitors from around the world met to recollect and remember, to sing and celebrate. The war had ended forty-five years earlier. This was the reunion of the Terezín inmates of 1942 to 1945. There were tears of sadness and joy.

Among these elderly people were the boys of Birkenau, with their wives and friends. Seventeen of us had spent part of our early teens – between July 1944 and January 1945 – in the family camp while the war raged and the Nazis carried out their murder of the Jewish people within our eyesight. There had been eighty-nine of us when Mengele selected us out of the *Familienlager* on July 6, 1944. Only thirty-five of us survived the war, and afterward we settled in all four corners of the world.

On May 6, 1990, we sat in a large room on the kibbutz and told our stories. The sun was shining as we stood up to talk about our past and present. It was a day full of joy and emotion. We talked about our lives and what we had done once freedom returned to us. We were all happy to be alive and together for this occasion. Most of us brought our wives and talked about our children and grandchildren. We talked about what we had achieved and said a prayer for those who did not survive. Then we returned to our hotel in the nearby town of Netanya. We spent the next few days at the sea or travelling throughout the beautiful country, admiring the sites and the people. For Nora and me, this was our seventh trip to Israel. This time, however, our emotions were especially strong because of the wonderful days we spent with our friends from the past. We pledged to meet again.

Glossary

Ančerl, Karel: (1908–1973) Renowned Czechoslovakian conductor; conducted for Prague radio 1933–1939. During the Holocaust, Ančerl was deported to Terezín and later to Auschwitz. After the war, he again conducted for Prague radio and then served as artistic director of the Czechoslovakian Philharmonic Orchestra for eighteen years. In 1968, Ančerl immigrated to Toronto, Ontario, where he conducted the Toronto Symphony Orchestra until his death in 1973.

Auschwitz: German name for Oświęcim [Polish], a town in southern Poland approximately thirty-seven kilometres from Krakow, and the name of the largest complex of concentration camps built nearby. The Auschwitz complex contained three main camps: Auschwitz I, a slave-labour camp built in May 1940; Auschwitz-Birkenau, a death camp built in early 1942; and Auschwitz-Monowitz, a slave-labour camp built in October 1942. In 1941, Auschwitz I was the testing site for the use of the lethal gas Zyklon B as a method of mass killing. The Auschwitz complex was liberated by the Soviet army in January 1945.

bar mitzvah: The age of thirteen, when a Jewish boy becomes religiously and morally responsible for his actions and considered an adult in synagogue ritual; also, a synagogue ceremony marking attainment of this status, with the boy called upon to read publicly from the Torah.

Beneš, Edvard: (1884–1948) Second and fourth president of Czecho-slovakia (1935–1938 and 1945–1948).

Blockälteste: [German] Prisoner appointed by the German authorities as barracks supervisor, charged with maintaining order and accorded certain privileges.

České Budějovice: [German: Budweiss] A small town in Southern Bohemia, Czech Republic, with a Jewish community recorded as early as 1867. During the interwar period, the town's Jewish population totalled just over one thousand.

Chanukah: [Hebrew: dedication; also Hanukah] An eight-day Jewish festival celebrated in December to mark the victory of the Jews against foreign conquerors who desecrated the Temple in the second century, BCE. The festival commemorates the rededication of the Temple and the miracle of its lamp burning for eight days without oil by lighting an eight-branch candelabrum called a menorah.

Family Camp/*Familienlager*: A special section of Auschwitz-Birkenau for Jews deported from Terezín in September 1943 and December 1943. The prisoners were forced to write postcards to family and friends still in Terezín to counter rumours of the Nazi annihilation of Jews. Many family camp prisoners were murdered in gas chambers on March 8 and 9, 1944; others were deported to slave-labour camps in July 1944; the rest were murdered on July 10 and 12, 1944, in the gas chambers.

February 1948 "Revolution": Non-violent seizure of power by the Communist Party in Czechoslovakia in February 1948, led by Communist leader Klement Gottwald, officially ending democratic rule.

Flossenbürg: The fourth concentration camp built in Germany, established in 1938. By the time it was liberated by the US army on April 23, 1945, 11,000 prisoners had been deported there. Three days before liberation, 14,000 prisoners were forced from Flossenbürg on a death march; on April 26, 1945, the survivors of the death march were retrieved by a US army unit.

ghetto: A confined residential area for Jews. The term originated in Venice, Italy in 1516, with a law requiring all Jews to live on a segregated, gated island known as Ghetto Nuovo. Throughout the Middle Ages in Europe, Jews were often forcibly confined to gated Jewish neighbourhoods. During the Holocaust, the Nazis forced Jews to live in crowded and unsanitary conditions in a dilapidated district of a city. Most ghettos were enclosed by brick walls or wooden fences with barbed wire.

Gymnasium: [Latin: school] An academic high school.

Gypsies: Common term for the Sinti and Roma, a nomadic people who speak Romany, an Indo-European language. Like the Jews, they were identified as an inferior race and targeted for genocide. In Auschwitz-Birkenau, over 20,000 Sinti and Roma were murdered; by war's end, between 250,000 and 500,000 had fallen victim to the Nazi genocide.

Kapo: A concentration camp prisoner appointed by the SS to oversee other prisoners as slave labourers.

kibbutz: Collectively owned farm or settlement in Israel governed democratically by its members.

Ma'oz Tsur: [Hebrew: Rock of Ages] A Jewish hymn traditionally sung after lighting the candles on the eight-branch candelabrum on the Jewish festival of Chanukah.

Masaryk, Jan (1886–1948): The son of Tomáš G. Masaryk, the founder and first president of Czechoslovakia. Educated in Czechoslovakia and the United States, Jan Masaryk served Czechoslovakia as ambassador to the United Kingdom until his country was overrun by the Germans in 1938. During World War II, Jan Masaryk served as foreign minister to the Czech government in exile, a position he retained in the provisional, multi-party National Front government established in Czechoslovakia following the liberation of his country from the Germans in 1945. In 1948, following a consolidation of a Communist, Soviet-led government, Jan Masaryk was found dead in his pyjamas in the courtyard of his apartment building. There is some debate as to whether he committed suicide as was proclaimed by the Communist government at the time or whether he was thrown to his death by Communist thugs.

Masaryk, Tomáš G.: (1850–1937) Considered the founder of Czechoslovakia and recognized as the head of the Czechoslovakian provisional government in 1918; first president (1920–1935); known for his strong public opposition to antisemitism.

Mengele, Josef: (1911–1979) Appointed SS garrison physician of Auschwitz in 1943, responsible for deciding which prisoners were fit for slave labour and which would be murdered immediately in the gas chambers; conducted sadistic experiments on Jewish and Roma prisoners.

Oranienburg (Sachsenhausen): A concentration camp located north of Berlin, Germany; established to imprison "subversive" elements.

Passover: A spring festival marking the exodus of the Israelites from Egypt and their liberation from slavery; an event commemorated by the seder, a ritual feast where the story is recounted, and by the eating of unleavened bread (matzah).

***Rollwagen Kommando*:** [German: truck unit] Concentration camp prisoners charged with loading, unloading and pushing a large wooden wagon.

***Sonderkommando*:** [German: special unit] Concentration camp prisoners charged with emptying corpses from the gas chambers, loading them into the crematoria and disposing of the remains.

SS: Short for Schutzstaffel, or Defense Corps, organized by Hitler in 1925 to protect him and other Nazi party leaders. Under the directorship of Heinrich Himmler, the SS developed into an elite corps whose members were selected according to racial criteria. SS membership grew from 280 in 1929 to 50,000 when the Nazis came to power in 1933 to nearly a quarter of a million on the eve of World War II. In 1934, the SS assumed most police functions including the Gestapo, the secret state police. The SS administered the concentration camps, persecuted Jews and suppressed political opponents through terror tactics.

Terezín: [German: Theresienstadt] A walled town in the Czech Republic sixty kilometres north of Prague that served as a ghetto between 1941 and 1945. From November 24, 1941, until March 30, 1945, 73,468 Jews from the German Protectorate (Bohemia and Moravia) and the Greater German Reich (including Austria and parts of Poland) were deported to Terezín, with the majority arriving in 1942. Terezín also served as a holding camp for "prominent" Jews, including decorated war veterans, artists and musicians, as well as orphans. More than 60,000 people were deported from there to Auschwitz or other death camps. Terezín was showcased as a "model" ghetto for propaganda purposes to demonstrate to delegates from the International Red Cross and others the "humane" treatment of Jews and to counter information reaching the Allies about Nazi atrocities and mass murder. The ghetto was liberated on May 8, 1945, by the Soviet Red Army.

Photographs

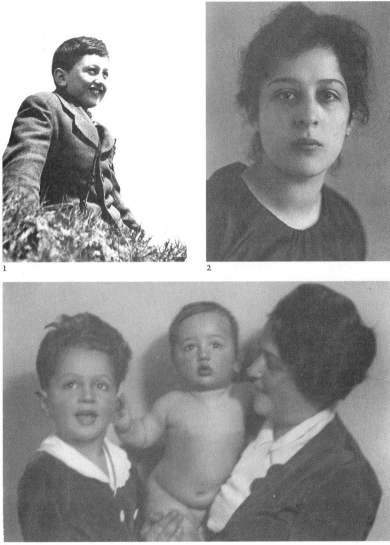

1 John at 10 years old (České Budějovice, 1941).
2 Erna Jung Freund, John's mother, at 19 years old (Pisek, Czechoslovakia, 1917).
3 John as a baby, mother Erna, and older brother Karel (České Budějovice, 1930).

1 Jewish children from John's hometown. Self-named *Solelim* (The Builders). John (far right) and boy second from left are the only survivors (České Budějovice, 1941).

2 John, about 10 years old (in front) with other Jewish children. Aside from John, the only survivor is the boy in the black shirt, whose mother was not Jewish (České Budějovice, 1940).

1 *Klepy* illustration featuring John and his favourite childhood pastime.
2 *Klepy* illustration featuring John's brother, Karel, and Susan Kopperl, the girl he
   liked. The text on the illustration reads, "You are the only one on the entire globe."
3 & 4 This page and the following two pages show copies from the original *Klepy*
   (Gossip) magazine. Each was hand-drawn and typed by John and his friends over
   the summers of 1940 and 1941. Original individual copies are held at the Jewish
   Museum in Prague/Židovské museum v Praze. The magazine's mission was "[...]
   to prove that a healthy spirit and sense of humour is within us and that we are
   not diminished by the difficulties of our days. We are capable, in moments of rest
   from our labour, to occupy our minds with worthwhile thoughts and humour."

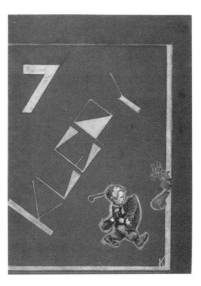

1 The building where John lived from birth until 1942. Photo taken by a friend
(České Budějovice, 1950).

2 John's father, Gustav, and mother, Erna (June 1941).

3 John (left), 11 years old, with his parents and older brother, Karel (c. 1941).

1 John's uncle Leopold Jung with his wife, Manja, and cousins Eva and Hannah (Prague, 1938).
2 Aunt Anna (Anda) from Austria (Prague, 1946).

1   John, 15 years old, at a swimming area (České Budějovice, 1945).
2   En route to Canada aboard SS *Aquitania*. (Left to right) Tom, Miriam and John (1948).
3   John, 18 years old (right) and friend Tomy Newman (left), aboard SS *Aquitania*, en route to Canada (March 1948). Tomy and John are still good friends.

1

2

3

1 John at his first job in front of Downy-Flake Doughnut shop on Sunnyside (Toronto, 1948).
2 John, 20 years old (Toronto, near Bathurst and College, 1950).
3 John and Aunt Anna, John's father's sister (Canada, 1959).

1 John and his wife, Nora (Toronto, 2007).
2 John (right) with grandchildren Jonah, Karly, Jack, Orlee, Michayla, Shira, Arielle, Gideon, Emily and Amanda and Daniel Bell (left), John's son-in-law (Canada, 2006).

Index

The Azrieli Foundation

The Azrieli Foundation was established in 1989 to realize and extend the philanthropic vision of David J. Azrieli, C.M., C.Q., MArch. The Foundation's mission is to support a wide spectrum of initiatives in education and research. The Azrieli Foundation is an active supporter of programs in the fields of Jewish education, the education of architects, scientific and medical research, and education in the arts. The Azrieli Foundation's many well-known initiatives include: the Holocaust Survivor Memoirs Publishing Program, which collects, preserves, publishes and distributes the written memoirs of survivors in Canada; the Azrieli Institute for Educational Empowerment, an innovative program successfully working to keep at-risk youth in school; and the Azrieli Fellows Program, which promotes academic excellence and leadership on the graduate level at Israeli universities.

Israel and Golda Koschitzky Centre for Jewish Studies

In 1989, York University established Canada's first interdisciplinary research centre in Jewish studies. Over the years, the Centre for Jewish Studies at York (cjs) has earned national and international acclaim for its dynamic approach to teaching and research. While embracing Jewish culture and classical study in all its richness, the Centre also has a distinctly modern core, and a strong interest in the study of the Canadian Jewish experience.

York was the Canadian pioneer in the study of the Holocaust. The Centre maintains its strong commitment to the study of the Holocaust through the research, teaching, and community involvement of its faculty, its graduate diploma program in Advanced Hebrew and Jewish Studies, and its unique program – developed in cooperation with the Centre for German and European Studies – for Canadian, German and Polish education students.